The Latino Holiday Book

3/03 ⓞ

Also by Valerie Menard

Cristina Saralegui: A Real-Life Reader Biography

Oscar De La Hoya: A Real-Life Reader Biography

Ricky Martin: A Real-Life Reader Biography

Salma Hayek: A Real-Life Reader Biography

Trent Dimas: A Real-Life Reader Biography

The Latino Holiday

BOOK

FROM Cinco de Mayo TO Día de los Muertos—

THE CELEBRATIONS AND

TRADITIONS OF

HISPANIC AMERICANS

Valerie Menard

FOREWORD BY CHEECH MARIN

MARLOWE & COMPANY
NEW YORK

TO MY PARENTS, JOE AND ELISA

Published by
Marlowe & Company
841 Broadway, 4th Floor
New York, NY 10003

THE LATINO HOLIDAY BOOK: *From Cinco de Mayo to Día de los Muertos—the Celebrations and Traditions of Hispanic-Americans*
Copyright © 2000 by Valerie Menard
Foreword copyright © 2000 by Cheech Marin

Library of Congress Cataloging-in-Publication Data

Menard, Valerie
    The Latino holiday book: from Cinco de Mayo to Día de los Muertos—
    the celebrations and traditions of Hispanic-Americans / Valerie Menard
        p. cm.
    ISBN 1-56924-646-7
    1. Festivals—United States. 2. Hispanic Americans—Social life and customs.

    GT4803 .M45 2000
    394.26'089'68073—dc21

                                                                    00-21889

9 8 7 6 5 4 3 2

Designed by Pauline Neuwirth, Neuwirth & Associates, Inc.

Printed in the United States of America

Distributed by Publishers Group West

Contents

4184-8672

WINTER • INVIERNO
Advent and a Fresh Start

Foreword

ONE OF MY earliest memories is of a crepe-paper-decorated shopping bag dancing above my head. The occasion was my fourth birthday and the shopping bag was my mother's homemade attempt at a *piñata*. A *piñata* in its most essential form is a big bag full of candy. This particular *piñata* was held up by a rope strung between two trees and manned by my slightly drunk uncle.

The drill went something like this: All the children were lined up and, one by one, blindfolded, spun around three times, and then handed a baseball bat and pushed in the direction of the dancing *piñata*. Between sips of beer, my uncle's job was to make sure that the *piñata* stayed somewhat intact until the birthday boy (me) got his turn. Somehow the blindfold would loosen, allowing a sneaky peek underneath, and magically the *piñata* would become almost still.

When I finally connected it was like a candy explosion, which was the cue for all the other kids to charge in like a wild mob. It was like an Easter egg hunt on steroids. Another slightly drunk and braver uncle had the job of grabbing me in the middle of my Mark McGuire impersonation so that the party would not end up at the emergency room.

The *piñata* is proof positive that Mexicans love their children more than anyone else. Who else would invent a game that combines the two things kids love most, candy and mayhem?

I won't even talk about the food and drink and music that followed. I will leave that to Valerie in her wonderful book that you should get to reading if only to find out just what the hell "Cinco de Mayo" really is.

Con Amor y Besos
CHEECH MARIN

CHEECH MARIN was for fifteen years half of the critically acclaimed, hilariously irreverent standup/music duo of "Cheech and Chong." With Tommy Chong he made eight feature films, and he has since appeared in a number of feature films and currently co-stars in the television drama *Nash Bridges*. The recipient of the 1999 National Council of La Raza/Kraft Foods ALMA Community Service Award on behalf of the Latino community, he continues to act, write, and direct, purvey a line of gourmet hot sauces, and build his collection of Chicano art, which is the largest owned by a private citizen.

Acknowledgments

IT TAKES a lot of help to write a book, and I would like to recognize the people who helped me complete this project. The staff at grassroots cultural organizations across the country provided invaluable information. From the Centro Cultural Aztlán in San Antonio to the Museo del Barrio in New York City, these organizations exist to ensure that Latino cultural traditions and history survive, even after generations of acculturation. I would like to thank the directors of all these groups for their help—many are cited in this book—and especially Father Michael Melendez of St. Michael's Parish in Flushing, New York, for his enthusiasm.

Many professors offered inestimable help, beginning with Gilberto Cardenas of the Inter-University Program for Latino Research at the University of Notre Dame. I've known Dr. Cardenas since his days as a sociology professor at the University of Texas at Austin (UT) and mine as an editor for *Hispanic*. Whenever I needed a Latino expert on any topic, he was the first person I called and he always led me to great people. For this book, he led me to Amelia Malagamba, professor of art history at UT, and Lisandro Perez at Florida International University. Thanks also to UT professor David Montejano and his referrals to professors Richard Flores, Jose Limon, and

Mauricio Tenorio, and to professor Federico Subervi for beginning my lesson on Puerto Rican culture.

Thanks to the librarians at the University of Texas at Austin Bensen Latin American Collection for building the university's holdings concerning U.S. Hispanics. When I was approached to do this book, I was encouraged to accept with the knowledge that this research library would hold a wealth of valuable information. Still, libraries remain undervalued, even at a university like UT, so I hope this commendation will afford librarians an opportunity to successfully request an expanded book and periodicals acquisition budget.

Thanks especially to Cheech Marin for agreeing to write the foreword and for confirming my theory that he is the nicest guy in Hollywood. To the authors cited in this book, who took the time to research the U.S. Latino culture for their own books, thanks for caring. *The Latino Holiday Book* is simply another contribution to an expanding library devoted to the discussion of U.S. Latinos and to educating people about this ancient and growing population.

Finally, thanks to my husband Reid, for his support, to my friends for their great ideas, to Melanie Cole for doing what she does so well, to Matthew Lore, my editor at Marlowe & Company, for his patience, and to my agent Laura Dail, for her great idea to do this book, for understanding the importance of cultural relevance on such a project, and for finding me. *Orale*, y'all.

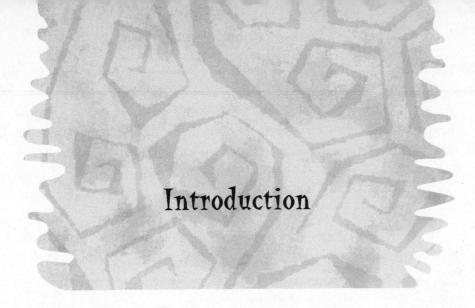

Introduction

HOLIDAYS SIGNIFY the good things in life. At the least, they mean a day off from work, and at the most, they offer a cherished opportunity to spend time with family and friends and connect with one's culture. Some holidays are more fun than others are, but depending on each family's traditions, one holiday usually carries more anticipation than the rest. For me that holiday would have to be Christmas. I'm an avowed Christmas nerd. Even though I get a little depressed when I see Christmas displays in September, I try to ignore them so that it won't spoil the Christmas spirit that comes rushing over me after Thanksgiving. My favorite Christmas tradition is decorating a Christmas tree. My motif is traditional—a fir tree bearing a hodge-podge of glass heirloom ornaments, new glittery ones that I buy after Christmas, and eclectic ones that I find to mark every vacation I've taken with my husband, from a sequined, felt English rose I bought in London to glittery seashells from the Texas coast to the big golden apple I bought in New York on our honeymoon.

As a second generation Mexican American, I also make a special effort to keep a cultural Christmas tradition alive—tamale making. I've spent the last six years under my mother's patient tutelage, practicing this age-old recipe in an exercise I called "tamale college." I've written down my mother's recipe, forcing her to measure ingredients she normally captures in her hand instead of a measuring spoon, following by heart the recipe that was passed down to her. I've put it on paper several times because I tend to lose them from year to year! But practice makes perfect, and I can now make them by heart just like my mother. I am a tamale college graduate.

When my agent, Laura Dail, approached me to write a book about Latino holidays, I jumped at the opportunity, not only because holidays mean a great deal to me but also because celebrations of my own culture renew warm ties with my family and friends. The Latino connection is important to me; indeed, my entire career as a writer has focused on the U.S. Latino community. From my first journalism position as managing editor of a Latino bilingual weekly paper in Austin, Texas, to my most recent job as senior editor with a national English-language magazine for Hispanics, my professional career has been linked to the Latino community. This experience has given me an invaluable and ongoing education about my own *raza* (people).

One of the first professional lessons I learned was that Hispanic media manages to combine advocacy and journalism. Because the mainstream media so often portrays our communities negatively, Hispanic media looks for positive, uplifting stories to provide a perspective on the Latino community that is rarely seen. Success stories, profiles of famous Latinos, and stories about Hispanic arts and culture all serve this objective. I personally know how negative stereotypes can tear at the heart and soul of an individual. I also know that only through education can society move forward.

The irresistible nature of the Latino culture has been revealed to mainstream culture through our food: salsa is now the number-one condiment in the United States, surpassing ketchup, and tortillas outsell white bread in many parts of the country. At the end of the twentieth century, Latin music and its stars were embraced overwhelmingly in this country. But there's much more to a community than its food and music. There's history, language, and tradition. Only through education can this country get better acquainted with the booming Latino population. Teachers know that the best way to teach a subject is to make it interesting and fun, so to achieve my goal of educating people on the history and traditions of the Latino culture, I thought, "What better way to do this than by discussing something fun like holidays?" Hence, my response to the offer of writing this book was, "I not only want to write this book—I must write it!"

As the first of its kind, this book is an overview of the holiday traditions of U.S. Latinos as they have evolved over several generations in this country. For that reason, this book focuses on the three largest ethnic groups within the Latino family in the United States: Mexican American (representing 64 percent of U.S. Latinos), Puerto Rican (11 percent), and Cuban American (4 percent). Because the history of the Mexican American community in this country predates the English Pilgrims, many of the holidays discussed in this book stem from that population's observances. The history of Cuban Americans and Puerto Ricans in this country, although not as long as Mexican Americans', also contains unique and fascinating traditions. These three Latino groups have the longest history in the U.S., and although there are books about certain Latin American holidays, no one has yet written a book on how these traditions were brought over by immigrants and then transformed by American culture.

Latino holidays have three main origins: culture, history, and religion. Although all the religious holidays discussed are Catholic, it is important to note that not every Latino is a member of the Catholic Church. However, the association with this religious denomination is pervasive, and its influence is still quite strong among the majority of Latinos.

I hope this book lets you in on some completely new ways to celebrate holidays. And I hope my book excites as well as informs. I'm proud to be a member of such a joyous and wise community. We have transcended our bittersweet history and have brought a little more color, liveliness, and soul to our *norte américa*. Thank you for taking the time to get to know us.

Bienvenidos

The Latino Holiday Book

SPRING

Celebrations of Renewal

∾

FIRST WEEK OF MARCH
CALLE OCHO

≋

FIRST SUNDAY AFTER VERNAL EQUINOX
(April or March)
EASTER

≋

MAY 5
CINCO DE MAYO

PRIMAVERA

LENT AND EASTER carry great significance within Christian communities. The climax of the forty-day fasting period of Lent–Easter Sunday–is considered the holiest Christian event, even more so than Christmas. According to the Christian Gospels, it was from the sacrifice of his own life that Christ saved the souls of all Christians. From Catholics to Presbyterians, the miracle of the resurrection of Christ binds each denomination together. Because so many Latinos are devout Christians, it is only natural that Easter is one of the most important celebrations of the year.

The spring message of rebirth is a joyous one, so many traditions associated with Easter take on that flavor. In Latin America, Easter is so revered that its celebration takes a whole week, called *semana santa*, and understanding employers usually comply by shutting down during that time. But most workers in the United States receive only one day off for Good Friday. Perhaps because they miss *semana santa*, Latino communities in the United States, such as Cuban Americans and Mexican Americans, add their own unique spin to this holiday season.

While all Latinos revere the religious rites of Lent and Easter, Cuban Americans in Miami hold the Calle Ocho festival right before Lent, around the second week in March, as a Latino turn on Mardi Gras. For Easter, Mexican Americans create *cascarones*, a fun twist on Easter eggs. And rounding out spring, Cinco de Mayo in May is a jubilant cultural celebration of victory over tremendous odds.

First Week of March
CALLE OCHO

Street Festival with a Salsa Beat

FORTY DAYS is certainly a long time to go without eating. But in the Christian tradition of Lent, the fasting period that cleanses the body of impurities is a metaphor for the cleansing of the soul that takes place on Easter. Over the centuries, this period has evolved into less of a fast and more of a time for Christians to ponder the meaning of sacrifice. Rather than a fast, worshipers now choose to "give up" something during Lent. It's not always food; it can be something they simply enjoy. Doing away with a favorite pastime, an indulgence, or food is a symbolic gesture to remind Christians of the sacrifice that Christ made to forgive their sins and save their souls.

But before this period of meditation and austerity, a period of *grande* indulgence is in order. Mardi Gras and Carnaval both evolved as big blowouts before Lent. The timing is similar for the Calle Ocho festival in Miami, but the objective of this festival is not just sensual enjoyment—it's also cultural affirmation.

CARNAVAL

For Latinos, the celebration known as Mardi Gras, or Fat Tuesday, is called Carnaval. The most famous Carnaval is held in Brazil, but Cuban Americans in Miami also celebrate a version of the holiday, called Calle Ocho (Eighth Street). This pre-Lenten party is named after the street that runs through the heart of Miami's Cuban community, known as Little Havana. At a Calle Ocho celebration in Miami, you can expect to indulge—before the purification and sacrifice required during the month-long observance of Lent—with salsa dancing, great Cuban food and drink, and music with *merengue* and *salsa* beats. *¡Salud!*

Savor the *Sabor*

Calle Ocho offers delicious food, hot rhythms, and spirited dancing—in this case, street salsa dancing. Sponsored by the Kiwanis Club of Little Havana, a nonprofit organization established in 1975, the weeklong celebration began as a fifteen-block-long party, with six performance stages for music and room for the 100,000 people who attended. By 2000, the event had stretched out to twenty-three blocks and included more than fifty musical stages, thirty stands, and an attendance of more than one million festivalgoers. It's a multicultural crowd: Miami's blue-and-green-striped buses deliver celebrants—Puerto Ricans, Dominicans, Colombians, black and white Americans—all singing, dancing, and ready to party.

Music takes center stage at the festival, from lesser-known Miami bands to top-billed acts like Celia Cruz, Gloria Estefan, and Arturo Sandoval. With the irresistible sounds of rumbas, mambos, and cha chas in the air, there's always room for dancing. Notes festival chairman José Marban, "Calle Ocho has become a little bit of everything. It's a combination of Mardi Gras and Carnaval." At Noche de Carnaval, the kickoff concert, the most famous Latino performers hold forth. Don't be surprised if the crowds form a *comparsa*—the famous Cuban line dance.

All the music and dancing makes revelers hungry, so along the street are vendors hawking Cuban delicacies like white rice, black beans, and pork, *tostones* (fried green plantains), *yuca, pinchos* (skewered beef) and *flan*. The festival has also evolved to reflect Miami's non-Cuban Caribbean population, so there is also Jamaican jerk chicken or Bahamian sweet potato pie to savor.

The history of Cuban Americans in this country dates back to the nineteenth century. Political conflicts with Spain brought the first group, and an ideological upheaval spurred the last. Cuban Americans have established themselves in Florida, and while many remain bonded to the island, more still wish to share their culture with their fellow Americans. Calle Ocho has become the main festival through which that wish has been realized.

The Birth of Little Havana

Since the Spanish American War, Cubans have immigrated to the United States in small numbers, but the rise of Cuban dictator Fidel Castro caused a rapid exodus from the island to Florida, particularly Miami. By 1960, thousands of Cubans had emigrated, escaping Castro's Communist regime. Most of these people were wealthy landowners, businessmen, and government officials who had been Castro's first targets after the revolution. Their property was seized and their jobs were forfeited. When they first arrived in Miami, they banded together in one area of the city that would eventually be called Little Havana.

The mentality of the exile differs from that of the immigrant. Cubans were forced to leave their country because of political, not economic, turmoil, and for that reason, the bonds to the island remain powerful, strengthened by a sense of nostalgia. Concern for loss of culture also encouraged the émigrés to recreate a Cuban lifestyle in the United States, which brought about the development of Little Havana and the street that runs through it, Calle Ocho. "The earliest cultural activities of Cuban émigrés resulted from their compulsive need to protect their *cubanía* (Cubanness) from the effects of the acculturation forces of American society," writes Miguel Gonzalez-Pando in his book *The Cuban Americans* (Greenwood Press: Westport, Connecticut, 1998). "Their earliest cultural manifestations simply reaffirmed the émigrés' sense of national identity in a foreign land."

Besides maintaining the culture, these Cuban émi-

World Beat on the World Wide Web

The Internet is a great place to look for information about the more established Latino holidays. In the case of Calle Ocho, the first page you should check out is **www.carnaval-miami.org**. At this site, you'll get the ins and outs of travel to and within Miami, events that are happening every day of the weeklong festival, and names of the hot acts that top off the celebration.

This home page is both visually and audibly appealing. An introductory movie asks the question: "What's ten days long, starts in Miami, ends in Latin America, has millions of feet, and dances to a salsa beat?" The answer, of course, is Carnaval. The Kiwanis-sponsored Web site helps users thoroughly understand the festival. It

grés were also concerned with regaining the wealth they had left behind. With its increasing economic prosperity, the Cuban community in Miami began to fund cultural and artistic activities. But a new wave of émigrés on the horizon and their fresh take on post-revolutionary Cuba would move Little Havana's cultural milieu in a new direction.

Los Marielitos

Twenty years after he assumed power, Castro felt the pressures of his closed-door policy toward the exiles in Miami. The country was struggling economically, and more and more Cubans felt compelled to join their families in the United States. In May 1980, Castro invited the exiles in Miami to come to Cuba and take back any Cuban who wished to leave. They were to collect this next round of émigrés at the port of Mariel, which is why the event became known as the "Mariel boatlift." The new arrivals to Miami were called *marielitos*. After five months of frenzied immigration, Miami's Cuban community had swelled in number by another 125,000.

The presence of this new population visibly changed Miami society. The image of Cuban immigrants would no longer be exclusively wealthy and successful. The *marielitos* were not wealthy in Cuba and brought less, financially, than had the first post-revolutionary wave in the 1960s. However, they did

explains that Carnaval Miami is held the first two weekends in March, beginning with Noche de Carnaval (Carnival Night) on the first Saturday. A star-studded program of international performers, bands, and dance groups entertain a large crowd at the Orange Bowl. This event is televised throughout the United States and Latin America.

Links within the site point you to special events planned for this year's celebration, such as "The World's Largest Cigar." You'll also find out what acclaimed artist won the Carnaval Miami Poster Contest, how to enter a cooking contest, how to get festival T-shirts and other souvenirs, where the Golf Classic and Calle Ocho fun runs are held, and much more.

Another information-filled site with information about Calle Ocho is **www.salsaweb.com**. At this site, which focuses on music and entertainment, you'll find descriptions of the musical offerings. One of the write-ups on the Web page describing the festival reads: "On Sunday is Calle Ocho. Eighth Street is blocked off from Fourth Avenue to Twenty-seventh Avenue. There are thirty stages—a large stage at each end and a stage at most intersections. Some of the most popular *salsa* and *merengue* bands and singers do several performances among the numerous stages. Performances at the Twenty-seventh Avenue stage are televised throughout the U.S. and Latin America. . . . Halfway along the route there are carnival rides and game booths. It all starts at noon, till 8 P.M., or until Oscar DeLeon stops playing."

So check out these and other sites for an eyeful and an earful of what the festival has in store.

bring a cultural temperament that would spur an artistic renaissance in Little Havana and cause the creation of Calle Ocho, the festival. "Among the 125,000 new refugees who came in that exodus were significant numbers of artists and intellectuals who had been raised under a revolutionary regime that placed much emphasis on the promotion of cultural activities," writes Gonzalez-Pando. "Their sudden arrival did more than inject a fresh dose of *cubanía* into the Cuban exile country; it added a rich cultural dimension to an emigrant community thus far characterized by the predominance of culturally apathetic, upper- and middle-class entrepreneurs and professionals."

Such established events as the Miami Book Fair International, the Miami Film Festival, and the International Hispanic Theater Festival have been credited to the *marielitos*. By 1978, Calle Ocho had gotten off the ground and was on its way to becoming the biggest Cuban cultural festival in the country.

EASTER

Cascarones Lighten Up the Holiday

AFTER THE pre-Lenten festivities of Carnaval and Calle Ocho comes Ash Wednesday, the first day of Lent. During Lent (from the Middle English word *lente,* meaning springtime), Roman Catholics, Orthodox Eastern Christians, and some Protestants observe forty weekdays of fasting and penitence. Rounding out this period, the celebration of Easter Sunday commemorates Christ's resurrection.

CASCARONES

The egg is the perfect symbol of renewal, befitting spring. When Easter comes, Latinos add a new twist to Easter-egg decorating and hunting—the Mexican *cascarón* (eggshell). Mexican American families take care to drain and clean whole eggshells at least a month before Easter, in order to create *cascarones*. Although the origin of these party eggs is undetermined, the practice has existed at least since near the turn of the twentieth century and has been passed on for generations in Mexico. Boiled Easter eggs are meant to be hidden by the Easter Bunny, found by children, and then eaten, but *cascarones*, which are filled with confetti and sealed with brightly colored tissue paper "hats," are meant to be cracked on people's heads!

A History of Egg Painting

Decorating Easter eggs is not a uniquely American custom, nor is its origin even Christian. Since ancient times, the egg has been the universal symbol of fertility and was used as part of the harvest ritual. The egg was also used as a positive object to ward off evil spirits. "Since the egg brings into existence new life, it was considered to be a talisman, a charm that averts misfortune and brings good luck. This property applied especially to the chicken egg, which contains the embryo of the solar bird—the rooster who announces the arrival of the sun every day and chases away evil spirits with his song," writes Zenon Elyjiw in a 1995 article in *The Ukranian Weekly*.

The simple egg has become an important symbol for many faiths, not just Christianity. It plays a key role in Jewish Passover traditions as well. The Judeo-Christian celebrations of Easter and Passover used to coincide; the celebrations were separated in A.D. 325 by the Council of Nicea. Since both are still calculated on a lunar calendar—Passover occurs on the first full moon after the spring equinox, while Easter occurs on the first Sunday after the first full moon of the vernal equinox—they may still coincide.

The exchange of eggs could have resulted as a by-product of Lent. In the first days of Christianity, no animal-derived foods could be eaten during Lent, especially eggs. However, that did not stop hens from laying them! As the supply of eggs grew, they were used for other purposes: to sanctify the land before plowing or planting or to ward off evil spirits, according to Edythe Preet in a March 31, 1999, *Washington Times* article. "By the time Lent ended, the piles of eggs had grown huge, and it became a tradition to break the long egg fast Easter morning with an egg feast," writes Preet. In the Middle Ages, crusaders witnessed an exchange of decorated eggs in the Holy Land and brought the custom of the egg feast home with them.

Egg painting became a popular art form in many parts of Europe, especially the Slavic countries, where decorated eggs are known for their intricate designs. Slavic eggs, called *psyanka,* are decorated using a batik technique, in which patterns are drawn on the egg with hot beeswax. Creating these striking patterns is a tedious process, requiring several applications of egg dyes followed by new beeswax designs in additional colors. After the artist has applied all the dyes and patterns required, the beeswax is melted off to reveal the pattern. But the patterns are not haphazard. They're based on ancient symbols and rituals. "The unusual beauty of the *pysanka* consists of the wealth and diversity of ancient symbols, which are arranged into attractive ornaments that enchant viewers with their composition, color scale, and their fascinating distribution on the curved and closed surface of the egg," writes Elyjiw.

Once the practice started, it was repeated each spring, usually borrowing the same motifs, which increased in importance over time. The patterns themselves became sacred. As talismans, the eggs took on a divine role, which made decorating them a sacred rite rather than a hobby. Only certain artists were allowed to decorate the eggs, which involved a ritual of prayer. Legend has it that during the ceremony, any bad or negative thoughts should be left outside because of their ability to counteract the talisman's positive strength. After the country's Christian conversion, "this old pagan spring custom was eventually accepted by the new religion and practiced in connection with the greatest Christian holiday of Easter," asserts Elyjiw.

Romanian Easter eggs, in addition to boasting the intricate beeswax designs, use a striking color—red. According to author Agness Murgoei, in a 1909 article in *Folklore* magazine, this practice is rooted in Christian tradition. The choice of color is connected to legends taken from Eastern Orthodox teachings. One legend has the color related to Christ's blood, which was said to have dripped on the eggs that were brought to him by his mother while he was on the cross. Another says that the eggs were used as projectiles, either by Mary and Joseph to protect themselves and the baby Jesus or by the Jews against Christ. A third legend is based on a feast of Jews celebrating Christ's death, which included boiled eggs. While joking about the promise of his resurrection, one reveler supposedly exclaimed that he would believe in Christ's resurrection when the cock they were eating rose from the dead and the eggs turned red, which then happened, according to the legend.

An interesting note in Murgoei's discussion is the mention of how the decorated eggs were used. The eggs are boiled during the dye process, but they are also broken. "Red eggs at Easter time is a Rumanian [sic] expression for inevitableness, as Easter without red eggs is unthinkable," she writes. "There are many customs in connection with the exchange or the breaking of the eggs. If two friends or relations wish to break eggs together, the younger one holds out an egg with the pointed end up and says, "Christ has risen.' The older one then strikes the young one's egg with the pointed end of his own egg, saying, "He has risen indeed.'"

Egg painting—and breaking—has a long and varied history. That Eastern European culture influenced egg-painting traditions in the Americas seems obscure, but there is a connection, across miles of ocean, land, and mountains, through the arrival of Christianity.

Easter Eggs, Latino Style

Like the red Romanian eggs, *cascarones* have been around for a long time. As yet, no one has accurately

How to Make Your Own *Cascarones*

Creating your own *cascarones* takes some advance planning. How many *cascarones* you end up with depends on how many eggs your household regularly uses and how soon you start saving the emptied eggshells. Follow these steps:

- **Save.** Starting at least a month in advance, every time you use an egg, it should be carefully broken from the narrow end, leaving as much of the oval eggshell intact as possible. (Since these eggs are not for decoration but for play, the use of an egg blower, which removes the yolk through a pinhole, is not necessary.) A hole approximately 1/2 inch in diameter is large enough to remove the egg's liquid contents as well as to insert confetti later.
- **Clean.** Prepare a soap bath for the empty shells. Swish through the soapy water and allow them to soak for a few minutes. Rinse well. After they are clean, let them air

dry, and store them in egg cartons.

⊛ **Decorate.** On the Saturday before Easter (Holy Saturday), your family can decorate the eggs as you would regular eggs—with PAAS Easter egg dye, glitter, paint, etc. Be very careful not to crack the delicate shells (it's a good idea to have a few extra on hand, just in case).

⊛ **Fill.** To fill the eggs, use pre-made confetti or make your own confetti by cutting bits of colored construction paper (the second option is the traditional one). Fill half full.

⊛ **Seal.** For egg covers, use brightly colored tissue paper. Cut out circles big enough to cover the open end of the egg. Apply glue around the rim of the egg and attach the tissue top so that it seals the opening without breaking. The seal should leave the egg with a small, flat top. Families can work in teams: one group concentrating on coloring and decorating the shells, the other group preparing the confetti and egg covers.

⊛ **Enjoy!** Remember, the purpose of making them is to break them on

dated when the practice began, but *cascarones* were mentioned in an 1897 catalogue published by the Folklore Society of London. In Mexico and the southwestern United States, they have been prepared and used to put more "celebration" into the solemn Easter holiday. All the same symbolism applies to *cascarones* as to any other Easter eggs: fertility, hope, and life.

Like their Eastern counterparts, the egg's contents are cleared and just the shell decorated to preserve the egg shape. They are no longer just utilitarian symbols for Easter; they have also taken on a social meaning. In the Ukraine, cracking hard-boiled eggs symbolized many things. In the ritual of tapping eggs, the person whose egg remains intact is said to have good luck for that year. Another version is that the egg represents Christ's tomb and that cracking the egg is a symbol of the tomb breaking open. Similarly, cracking *cascarones* over the head could have had many meanings. The act could symbolize the opening of the tomb, or it could also be a reenactment of efforts to awaken Christ so that he can rise to save humankind. Whatever the reason, painting the eggs, filling them with confetti, and topping them with a tissue paper cap is unique to Mexico and Mexican Americans.

Since the end product of *cascaróne*-making is fun, the decoration of *cascarones* is not usually as laborious as that of other Easter eggs around the world. Although they can be pastel blues, yellows, and pinks, most *cascarones* are brightly colored. Any medium will do—dyes, acrylic paint, glitter—whatever is handy. They often feature flowers, animals, rainbows, flags, or any other symbol that has meaning to the decorator.

Writer Yleana Martinez remembered her family's Easter tradition, which included *cascarones*, in a March 1996 article in *Hispanic* magazine: "Growing up in South Texas, my siblings and I awakened on warm spring mornings for the egg hunt. Barefooted and in pajamas, we'd race outside, first to search for the basket left by La Coneja (the Easter Bunny), then to collect the *cascarones* we decorated in the days leading up to Easter. . . . Woe to the child who carelessly smashed some of his or her precious arsenal, for that was how we regarded our *cascarones*. . . . After Mass, the family would drive to a ranch for a reunion and the traditional *carne asada*. Just before sundown, we'd get the signal from a grown-up that the moment had arrived. All manners and civility were lost as everyone chased each other around, smashing dozens of painted eggshells on delicate craniums."

someone's head. Picnics are great places to use *cascarones*, or perhaps during an Easter egg hunt. The fun of *cascarones* is the element of surprise. If used correctly, they should be exciting, not painful. Never use them as projectiles. Hold the *cascaróne* in the palm of your hand and then seek out a victim. Sneak up behind your target and smash the *cascaróne* on his or her head quickly but not forcefully. It doesn't take much to break an egg, much less its empty shell.

Once they're cracked—and smothered into the victim's hair—the *cascarones'* confetti and eggshell shards fly around with abandon amid peals of laughter.

CINCO DE MAYO

Victory Against All Odds

THE ATTRACTION to Cinco de Mayo in the United States isn't hard to understand. Cinco de Mayo almost always means a huge fiesta, with the attendant food, music, and dancing to attract a multicultural audience. The holiday has become so popular on this side of the border that a U.S. Postal Service stamp was issued to commemorate the occasion.

Besides being a big party, Cinco de Mayo offers a chance to immerse yourself in Mexican American culture. Experiencing this culture by attending a Cinco de Mayo celebration means watching the color and excitement of *ballet folklórico* dancers, cheering to irresistibly upbeat *mariachi* tunes like

"Guadalajara" and "Jalisco," and savoring such Mexican culinary delights as *gorditas* (thick corn tortillas sliced like a pita and stuffed with lettuce, tomato, beef, chicken, or cheese) and *buñuelos* (deep-fried pastries topped with cinnamon and sugar). But what in fact is everyone celebrating?

THE MOST MISUNDERSTOOD HOLIDAY

Cinco de Mayo may be the most familiar yet misunderstood Latino holiday. Many in this country assume that May 5 is the celebration of Mexico's independence from Spain, just as July 4 is the celebration of our independence from Britain. In fact, May 5 does not signify independence from Spain—September 16 does. What Cinco de Mayo does signify is an important David-versus-Goliath battle in Mexican history. Because of the late spring occurrence of the holiday, Cinco de Mayo celebrations take place nationwide at the end of the school year, allowing everyone—not just Latinos—to revel in the dance (*ballet folklorico*), music (*mariachi, conjunto*), and food (tacos, *gorditas, buñuelos*) of Mexico.

An Unexpected Victory Alerts a Nation

Contrary to what many believe, Cinco de Mayo does not celebrate Mexican independence but rather a battle between a small Mexican army and a large French army. In 1862 General Ignacio Zaragoza successfully led his small force of four thousand men against twice as many French soldiers to defeat the larger French army in the city of Puebla. Because of the David and Goliath theme of this battle, it is remembered by Mexicans and Mexican Americans as a striking example of determination, courage, and ingenuity against overwhelming odds. The victory did not lead directly to Mexican independence because the French occupation, which followed forty years of freedom for Mexico from Spanish rule, intensified after this battle. But five years after the Battle of Puebla, Mexico did finally manage to gain permanent independence.

Independence for Mexico was not achieved quickly or easily. Unlike the United States, which once it achieved independence from Britain never lost it, Mexico changed hands several times and struggled through a civil war before finally settling into its sovereignty. The Battle of Puebla, which is the backdrop for Cinco de Mayo, took place before the Mexican Revolution, when the country was under a brief occupation by the French and was trying to rebuild after the Mexican-American War of 1846–48.

In 1861, Mexico had just recovered from its own internal struggle to lessen the control held over it by the Catholic Church. Benito Juárez had just taken over as president, but the country owed money to England, Spain, and France. Juárez called a moratorium on repayment of debts to these nations. Spain and England solved the issue with Mexico through diplomatic methods, but France had other needs it wanted satisfied, and an emperor willing to pursue them: Ferdinand Maximilian von Hapsburg.

Second in line to the Austrian-Hungarian throne, von Hapsburg had the desire to rule but not the means. While his older brother, Franz Joseph, was being groomed to take the throne, Maximilian spent much of his time traveling to nearby locations like Spain but also to distant destinations like Brazil. He was an emperor wannabe without a country, but because the Mexican Reform was having difficulty taking root and many of the exiled Mexican aristocracy maintained visions of establishing a Mexican empire, an opportunity arose for Maximilian. Napoleon III was in control in France, and with his wife, Eugenia de Montijo, they shared an immense interest in taking control of Mexico. A Spaniard, Eugenia saw a Mexican Empire as a means of taking revenge for Spain, which the Mexicans had defeated forty years earlier. For Napoleon, establishing a presence in Mexico would maintain France's foothold in North America and possibly create a chance to take advantage of a weakened United States caught up in the Civil War.

So French forces invaded Mexico, and except for a few losses like the one suffered in Puebla, the takeover was a success. Exiled president Benito Juárez abandoned Mexico City, although he maintained control of Northern Mexico throughout the French occupation. On April 10, 1864, Maximilian accepted the throne and crown of Mexico, but his reign lasted only three years.

A Clever Cattle Ploy

At the Battle of Puebla, the well-trained French army came up against the wits of a nation back on its heels. Maximilian's French dragoons met General Zaragoza and Colonel Porfirio Díaz (who would eventually become Mexico's most infamous president) and their troop of Mexicans and Zapotec and *mesti-zo* Indians. Zaragoza sent Díaz and the renowned Mexican cavalry to meet the French flanking army. The French cavalry followed suit, leaving only the infantrymen in position in the center of the battle. In an ingenious maneuver, Zaragoza released a heard of stampeding cattle ahead of his infantry to act as a buffer and to splinter the French forces, which it did most effectively.

The victory at Puebla did not end the French invasion, but to many it marked the beginning of the end of foreign control of Mexico. *Corridos* of the battle inspired hope in the populace throughout the five-year French occupation until Maximilian eventually surrendered in May of 1867. By then, he had no choice. The continued resistance by the Mexican people and their president-in-hiding, Juárez, took a financial toll on France. On January 15, 1866, Napoleon III decided to end the occupation and withdraw his troops. Maximilian's wife and principal advisor, Carlota, returned to Europe and eventually to her native Belgium. Maximilian surrendered more than a year later. On June 19, 1867, he and his generals were executed by firing squad. Mexico's occupation by a foreign power had finally ended.

Cinco de Mayo Takes Off

The popularization of Cinco de Mayo as a cultural celebration did not happen overnight. It was a gradual process that one scholar suggests began in the United States, at about the time of the French invasion of Mexico, with Mexicans in California (or what was northern Mexico at the time), as a way of showing solidarity with their mother country.

Using San Francisco's Latino community as a case study, researcher Laurie Kay Sommers breaks down the evolution of Cinco de Mayo into three stages. She cites an article published in a San Francisco Latino community newspaper, *La Voz de Mejico,* on May 26, 1862, which discusses the battle at Puebla. The following year, while Mexicans continued to resist the French occupation, a Mexican entrepreneur began a Cinco de Mayo dance. This first phase, writes Sommers in a 1984 article published in the *Journal of American Folklore,* continued through the 1950s and maintained the same format—private dances organized by various Mexican civic and social clubs. Civic elements of the celebration included speeches about the significance of the day, a parade with floats, and *folklórico* dances from Spain and Mexico performed by area dance troupes. The celebrations remained local and contained within a city's Mexican American community.

But all that changed in the 1960s and 1970s. A tumultuous decade, the sixties brought much constructive change for people of color through the Civil Rights movement. Like the African American community, the Latino community in the United States began to demand equality and to fight against all forms of discrimination—in school, on the job, or even at the grocery store. From this growing self-awareness grew the Chicano movement, an effort by Mexican Americans to reembrace their indigenous roots and recognize the struggle of native peoples in Mexico against the Spanish conquistadors and other European invaders. The momentum of the Civil Rights movement carried the Chicano movement from the sixties into the seventies.

According to Sommers, it was at this time that Chicanos began to search for a celebration that would reflect their experience and history in the United States. Likewise, educators, who were not unaffected by the Civil Rights movement, became more and more aware of the importance of incorporating culturally relevant topics into school curricula. For both groups, Cinco de Mayo fit the bill.

The event falls near the end of the school year, in the spring, so it was more appealing to educators than the true celebration of Mexican independence on September 16 (*diez y seis de septiembre*), which takes place at the very beginning of the school year. This gave teachers more time to prepare activities for the celebration and provide their students with classroom instruction. The Cinco de Mayo initiative gained even more momentum in 1968 with the passage of the Bilingual Education Act, which dramatically increased federal funding for multicultural curricula.

For Chicanos, the date held more appeal than September 16 did because of its symbolism and message. The Mexican army was considered bold, empowered by its desire for independence, and its victory became a classic example of self-determination. Labeled a minority in the United States, Chicanos could relate to the outnumbered Mexican forces, and although their struggle had just begun, Chicanos hoped to emulate the same success in battle. Also, the fact that General Zaragoza was born in the part of Mexico that became Texas linked the battle more closely to the experience of Mexicans in the United States, whereas September 16 was a significant date in Mexico but had no connection to the United States.

The combination of education and increasing publicity helped position Cinco de Mayo as the premiere Mexican American celebration. In the 1980s, when corporate America began to look at the growing number of Hispanic consumers and consider ways of appealing to them, Cinco de Mayo provided the perfect avenue. Many celebrations were organized by community-based organizations, which welcomed financial assistance to underwrite their event. In exchange for their financial support, corporations got what they wanted— increased visibility and a positive image in the Latino community. Once national marketing campaigns took control, Cinco de Mayo became an American holiday.

The Celebration Today

Hispanic communities nationwide continue to organize public celebrations of Cinco de Mayo as a cultural and educational tool. Although these groups recognize that the date is still confused with September 16, the real Mexican Independence Day, they feel that the story behind Cinco de Mayo still carries historical significance. The fact that the date was so readily embraced by most Americans doesn't hurt either.

In the Texas town of San Marcos, Cinco de Mayo holds great importance. A local civic group has devoted an extensive Web site to the celebration, **www.vivacincodemayo.org**. This Web page links to other sites built by groups all over the country. Sponsored by the local chapter of the League of United

Latin American Citizens (LULAC), the site offers the history of the event, photos of past celebrations, a map to San Marcos, a list of events, which includes a *menudo* (a soup made of tripe, hominy, and red chile) cookoff and recipe, and a low-rider festival.

From this site, you can link to information about Cinco de Mayo celebrations in San Jose, universities around the country, Washington, D.C., and even a tree company in Oregon, J. Frank Schmidt and Son. According to the company's Web site, Cinco de Mayo "has become a favorite tradition at our company. It's a day on which we honor our hard-working, dedicated production employees who are primarily of Mexican heritage."

The event billed as the largest Cinco de Mayo celebration in the country is the AT&T Fiesta Broadway in Los Angeles, California. Established in 1989, the daylong festival spans thirty-six square blocks in downtown Los Angeles and attracts 300,000 participants. Its main attractions are musical performances by popular and unsigned Latino bands, as well as such family-oriented activities as a children's art workshop, a World Cup sports center, and a health expo. According to Fiesta literature, the event is "dedicated to the working Latino family that looks forward to commemorating their heritage and traditions in a cultural, artistic, and safe environment on the famous downtown Los Angeles Broadway corridor."

The event's original impetus, however, came from the private sector, namely the national Spanish-language network, Univision. The network had already enjoyed success with its support of the Calle Ocho festival in Miami and wanted to recreate that type of event in Los Angeles. Realizing that the focus would have to represent the Hispanic community in Los Angeles much like Calle Ocho, which has a strong Cuban theme, represented the community in Miami, Univision turned its attention to Cinco de Mayo.

"L.A. Fiesta Broadway was born in the city of Los Angeles, which has the largest Latino population in the United States. We were looking for an event that recognized the rich contributions that the Mexican American culture has made to the city and that also brought together the broader community. We felt the Cinco celebration could accomplish those two goals because the most efficient and nonthreatening way to break down barriers is through music, food, and culture," explains Larry Gonzalez, a former employee with Univision and currently president of All Access Entertainment. At the time, the network approached then-mayor Tom Bradley to sign up the city as cosponsor of the event. With the city's support, permits for closing streets like Broadway and policing of the event were provided. Still very much a private venture, the event pursues sponsors like AT&T to cover its budget of more than $1 million.

Besides its seven music stages, L.A. Fiesta Broadway also includes food booths that, as with smaller festivals in other parts of the country, have been reserved for nonprofit-group fundraisers. For example, one year, Roosevelt High School was granted all soda refreshments to raise money for the school. There's also an educational element to the event—an art and essay contest in which all area students are invited to participate. In 1998, more than 15,000 students submitted their work. The winners of the contest have their creations featured at the festival and also receive a U.S. savings bond.

L.A. Fiesta Broadway takes place on the last Sunday in April and is free to the public. To encourage the family-friendly environment of the event, no liquor is sold there.

For event planners like Gonzalez, Cinco de Mayo has important cultural significance for Mexican Americans, and that needs to be unmistakable for any

Simple Cinco Margaritas

1 six-ounce can of frozen limeade
4 shots of tequila
ice
salt (optional)
fresh limes

This may be the simplest recipe for margaritas, but it's also the most foolproof. Fill a blender with ice. Add the tequila and the can of limeade. Blend together until most of the ice chunks have been crushed.

For margaritas with salt, cover a small plate with loose salt. Dampen the rim of a margarita glass with a paper towel. Dip the glass—rim first—into the plate of salt. Then pour in the margarita mixture. Garnish each 'rita with a slice of lime.

event. "Cinco de Mayo celebrations are very much a product of the Chicano movement and were popularized by Latinos in California," offers Gonzalez. "But it has also reached areas like New York and Miami, where it has become as mainstream as St. Patrick's Day. It's important that these communities also understand the significance of Cinco de Mayo and what the battle represented."

Today Cinco de Mayo celebrations vary from eating Mexican food at a local restaurant and toasting the day with margaritas, to attending an outdoor event or fiesta, usually held at a city-owned park located in the heart of a Hispanic neighborhood. At these fiestas be prepared to hear music, usually *mariachi* or *conjunto*, watch *folklórico* dancers, and sample delicious examples of Mexican cuisine. They are excellent opportunities for families, offering a variety of activities for children, from paper-flower–making to carnival rides. Recognizing the date's historical importance, many celebrations also feature an education program and speeches by elected officials. Taking advantage of the event's opportunity for cultural pride, competitions such as beauty contests and low-rider car shows are also favorites. The evening usually ends with a dance or concert.

Although it has become commercialized, Cinco de Mayo still holds great cultural and historical significance to many U.S. Hispanics. The concept of political freedom certainly strikes a chord as well. If you and your family opt to join in the celebration, be aware that Cinco de Mayo is much more than a just good excuse to party. It's also a chance to reflect on the value of freedom and the character of a people who held on to their country against all odds.

SUMMER

Life Celebrations and Political Holidays

～

MAY 10
CUBAN INDEPENDENCE DAY

～

JUNE 24
FEAST OF SAN JUAN BAUTISTA

～

SECOND SUNDAY IN JUNE
NATIONAL PUERTO RICAN DAY (U.S.)

～

SEASONAL
QUINCEAÑERAS, BIRTHDAYS, AND WEDDINGS

VERANO

SUMMER FIESTAS, from the celebration of Cuban Independence to the Puerto Rican Day Parade, find Latino communities commemorating both their political history and their modern reality. Three fiestas take place between May and June, celebrating the heritage of two Caribbean Latino cultures: Cuba and Puerto Rico. These three festivals—Cuban Independence Day, the Feast of San Juan Bautista (St. John the Baptist), and Puerto Rican Day—bring early summer good times to U.S. cities with sizable Caribbean populations.

Every May 20, Cubans remember their independence from Spain, which occurred in 1902 after U.S. troops, which had occupied the island since the end of the Spanish American War on December 10, 1898, left. June 24 ushers in the Feast of San Juan

Bautista, celebrated by Puerto Ricans. Puerto Ricans also put on the Puerto Rican Day Parade on the second Sunday in June, to show cultural pride more than to celebrate "independence." For the most part, these holidays are celebrated only in places with high Cuban and Puerto Rican populations, such as Miami and New York. If you get the chance to attend one of them, you'll learn about the Caribbean culture not just from the music and tasty cuisine but also from thought-provoking occasions such as awards ceremonies and masses, which also honor each island's history in their way. Cultural and historical holidays such as these provide important clues to the attitude and perspective of a community—plus, they're delicious!

Summer is also a traditional time for weddings, and this section describes the deep cultural roots behind three life celebrations practiced with gusto by U.S. Latinos: weddings, birthdays, and *quinceañeras*. As with most other special occasions, Latinos give a special turn to these milestones in family life. More and more, second and third generations of Latinos are embracing traditional elements of these life celebrations.

CUBAN INDEPENDENCE DAY

Historic and Ongoing Struggle

CUBA'S STORY of independence is joyful or tragic, depending on which Cuban American you talk to. Many émigrés from the 1959 revolution vow never to return to the island until Castro leaves office or dies, whichever comes first. As new generations of Cuban Americans born in the United States establish themselves, it's up to the older generation to remind them what it was like to grow up in Cuba. Celebrating Cuba's independence is one way to do that.

Although it is an important event, the celebration has become fairly low key, says Carlos Verdecia, editor of *Hispanic* magazine. The first celebrations involved parades, but they have evolved into ceremonies of recognition. "Basically the attitude for Cubans is, independence is a moot point," says Verdecia. The observance usually takes the form of a dinner or reception at which speeches are made, recognizing that the struggle for independence in Cuba continues. The appeal for this event is definitely among members of the first post-revolution exodus, says Verdecia. "The twentieth of May is still important to many Cubans; however, in the year 2002, on the centennial celebration of Cuban independence, the celebrations will be greater." To appreciate the holiday is to know the country's history.

A Continuing Struggle for Freedom

It took Christopher Columbus two weeks after first making landfall in the Dominican Republic on October 12, 1492, to "discover" Cuba. When he sailed up a large river in Cuba, he remarked in his notes, "[I've] never beheld so fair a thing; trees all along the river, beautiful and green and different from ours, with flowers and fruits each according to their kind, and little birds which sing very sweetly." At the time, there were native people on the island, although not the Oriental civilizations Columbus expected to find. They were Guanahatabey, Ciboney, Taino, and Arawak. The most aggressive tribe, the Karib, for whom the Caribbean region was named, were on the verge of a takeover of the island from the other natives, but the Spanish arrived before it could be completed.

Initially, Cuba served as a central location for forays to the rest of Latin America. Columbus built a home in nearby Hispaniola (present-day Haiti and the Dominican Republic), and although Spain concentrated its colonization efforts from Hispaniola, it was only a matter of time before the focus would switch to Cuba. It didn't take long for the indigenous population to be depleted in Hispaniola, along with the island's supply of gold. "Spain began looking for new conquests. Not surprisingly, they cast their gaze across the Windward Passage to Cuba," write James and Judith Olson in their book, *Cuban Americans: From Trauma to Triumph* (Twayne Publishers: New York, 1995). The Spanish commissioned Sebastián de Ocampo to explore the rest of the island, and in 1508 he became the first European to circumnavigate Cuba.

Because gold was much more plentiful in Mexico and Peru, Cuba remained a farming community and Spain began importing African slaves there in 1523. Still, population growth on the island was slow. Spanish women were in short supply, and by the seventeenth century, Spanish men began mixing with Indian and African women. By then, the island also held a growing population of free blacks, since sugar production was not as intense as it was in other parts of the Caribbean. These freed slaves eventually made up a large portion of Cuba's working class.

Tobacco, cattle, and sugar production grew, but in the eighteenth century production of these crops exploded with the economic reforms of Charles III in Spain. He lifted trade restrictions and divested local monopolies, which spurred Cuba's economy and also elevated the position of the island's *criollo* (Cuba-born Spaniard) population. "*Criollo* political consciousness, fueled by the new prosperity as well as continuing domination of the Cuban military, church, and bureaucracy by *penninsulares* [Spaniards], sharpened even more," write the Olsons. Even so, by the nineteenth century, when most Spanish colonies had begun to break free, Cuba remained loyal to the crown.

Latin American leaders such as Juaquín Infante, José Francisco Lemus, and Simón Bolívar made early efforts to incorporate Cuba into the revolutionary movement, but they were quickly stifled. This activity did send some of the first Cuban exiles to the United States. Felix Varela y Morales, for example, fled to New York after facing arrest for his proposed reforms. The real revolutionary spark would not burst into flame until 1868, in an uprising led by Carlos Manuel de Céspedes. A *criollo,* Céspedes was a successful sugar planter who launched the Ten Years' War when he declared independence from Spain on October 10, 1868. This date is still a national holiday in Cuba.

Although influential leaders like José Martí and Antonio Maceo y Grajales joined up with Céspedes, Spain eventually prevailed, squelching the rebellion. The seed of freedom, however, had been sown. Martí continued his campaign for independence, writing newspaper articles and organizing overt protests in the United States among the growing number of Cuban émigrés. "Because of the severe economic problems in Cuba during the 1880s and early 1890s, large numbers of people emigrated from the island," write the Olsons. "Thousands of them settled in the United States. Between the 1840s and the 1890s separatist thought among Cuban Americans evolved from an economic liberalism envisioning annexation to the United States to envisioning absolute Cuban independence, complete with vast social and economic change."

Another national holiday related to Cuba's independence is February 24, the date in 1895 when Martí issued the call to arms against Spain and headed back to Cuba, joined by his compatriots and thousands of exiles. Rather than taking a philosophical approach, this time the rebels took up arms. They focused their aggression on the plantation owners, burning all their crops. Martí died in battle that same year, but the rebellion continued for three more years.

In 1898, Spain's presence in the Caribbean faced its end when the *U.S.S. Maine* exploded in Havana harbor. Although it's unclear what caused the explosion aboard the ship, the sinking of a U.S. battleship and the loss of 252 sailors brought the United States into the conflict, upgrading the Cuban–Spanish struggle to the Spanish American War.

Weakened by thirty years of resistance from Cuba and its other colonies, Spain capitulated within months. The United States received huge dividends for its eight-month struggle with Spain. At the Treaty of Paris, which ended Spanish control in the Caribbean, the United States paid Spain $20 million and received Guam and Puerto Rico. Cuba received its independence but not immediately. Fearing for the safety of the many U.S. business interests in Cuba and concerned about the island's proximity to Florida, the United States occupied Cuba between 1898 and 1902.

The American occupation transformed Cuba's economy. According to the Olsons, American companies didn't hesitate to expand operations onto the island, so that by 1906 they owned 20 percent of the island and 75 percent of the cattle ranches. Spaniards also retained their control under the Treaty of Paris, which guaranteed their land rights. The United States also influenced political development in Cuba, requiring adoption of the Platt Amendment—which allowed future intervention by the United States on the island—before approving the first Cuban constitution. "Thus began the U.S. occupation of the former Spanish colony, a difficult and complex period of transition during which most Cubans feared their quest for sovereignty would be compromised by the imperialist designs of the 'Northern Colossus,' " writes Miguel Gonzalez-Pando in *The Cuban Americans* (Greenwood Press: Westport, Connecticut, 1998).

But on May 20, 1902, the U.S. occupation ended and the island elected its first president, Don Tomás Estrada Palma. American involvement on the island, especially its support of the dictator Fulgencio Batista, would eventually lead to Cuba's fateful revolution more than fifty years later. During this revolution in 1959, Fidel Castro installed himself as the country's new dictator.

WHO WAS JOHN THE BAPTIST?

As the first Christian martyr, Saint John has a tragic story in the Gospels. John the Baptist was Jesus's cousin. He was born six months before Jesus, on June 24, his feast day. His birth was a near miracle because his mother had never borne children and had assumed that she was barren. She gave birth to John after she had already experienced menopause. As he grew up, John became a prophet, telling of his cousin's arrival. He popularized the practice of baptizing his followers by dunking them in water and baptized Jesus in the River Jordan.

John made enemies of King Herod and his wife, Herodias, however, when he criticized the king for marrying his brother's wife while his brother was still alive. Herod held a large party, at which his niece, Salome, performed "a very pleasing dance." Herod was so overwhelmed by her performance that he told Salome she could have anything. After consulting with her mother she asked for the head of John the Baptist. The king granted her wish, presenting her the Baptist's head on a platter.

LOW-KEY POLITICAL EVENTS

Independence is a sore spot for many Latinos who have Puerto Rican or Cuban roots. The most important thing to remember in regard to the Puerto Rican perspective is that they really have no Independence Day to celebrate. Although the country was freed from Spanish rule, the island swapped a colonial ruler, Spain, for a commonwealth guardian in the form of the United States. Puerto Rico has never experienced true political autonomy.

With Cuban Americans, the issue is also sensitive. Most Cuban Americans have not resolved the concept of independence, largely because many of them view their "freedom" as compromised by the control of Communist dictator Fidel Castro over their homeland. These celebrations are not widespread across the country, but they are a boon for the lucky residents of the regions where they are held. To sample great

food, dance, and music, and learn more about another culture,

get out and attend one of these festivals.

FEAST OF SAN JUAN BAUTISTA

Patron Saint of Puerto Rico

THE FEAST of San Juan Bautista is a national holiday in Puerto Rico, but one without a day off of work. Considering when the celebration takes place, no one should have to work the next day. Practically en masse, the country heads to the beach on or before midnight for the celebration of San Juan Bautista. It's a party atmosphere certainly, but there is a serious ritual also. Bathers head into the ocean backwards and then come out of the water at least three times. This action may symbolize rebirth, but locals believe it has more to do with casting off evil or negative energies. The celebration is not practiced exclusively on the island. It has migrated up the Atlantic seaboard and is carried on by New York Puerto Ricans, or *nuyoricans,* in the past on Randall's Island in the Bronx, and today in Central Park.

When Christopher Columbus landed on the island now called Puerto Rico, he decided the port of riches shared a kinship with John the Baptist and christened the island San Juan Bautista de Puerto Rico. Why exactly he chose this name may be more a matter of habit than inspiration. The Catholic Church dominated Spain and would soon dominate Spanish colonies in the Americas. Father Miguel Meléndez of Saint Michael's parish in Flushing, New York, and adjunct professor at St. John's University, postulates, "It was the custom to name places discovered by Spanish explorers after the saints. You see this pattern throughout Latin America." Indeed, in Puerto Rico, each town boasts a patron saint and celebrations of the saints' feast days are common.

The symbolism of dunking themselves in the water may be obvious to most Catholics as a direct representation of baptism. Since 1955, Puerto Ricans in New York have held their own version of the San Juan Bautista festival. The festival begins at ten in the morning and lasts until six in the evening, at Dewitt Clinton Park between Fifty-second and Fifty-fourth Streets. At one o'clock, a procession that features a statue of the saint makes its way to the Archbishop for a blessing. It's followed by a mass. Afterward, there is an awards ceremony in which the medallion of John the Baptist is presented to an outstanding community leader. Once the formalities are out of the way, the fiesta begins, replete with music, dance, and food from the island.

Puerto Rico's Early Days

Christopher Columbus came across the island on his second journey to the Americas in 1493. Like the Dominican Republic, where he first landed, a native population inhabited the island. In Puerto Rico's case, this group was a gentle people known as the Tainos. An agricultural community, the Tainos posed little opposition to the Spanish invaders who followed. The Tainos were not equipped to resist the invasion physically. The native population dwindled quickly, decimated by slave labor and disease. This rapid decline of the Tainos caused the Spaniards to introduce African slaves into the Caribbean diaspora mix.

Puerto Rico was colonized fifteen years after Columbus's first landing by Juan Ponce de Leon, who again christened the land San Juan Bautista and named the capital city Puerto Rico (rich port). Eventually the names were reversed—San Juan became the capital and Puerto Rico became the name for the island.

Spain kept a tight grip on the island even after its limited gold deposits had been depleted. Puerto Rico became important for its climate, which produced prolific agricultural ventures. In 1522, the King of Spain became concerned that the island might fall into the hands of the British, so he ordered the construction of several strategic forts to protect against an invasion. The largest of these Spanish forts, El Morro Castle, faces the ocean and protects the city of San Juan.

Puerto Rico and Cuba remained under Spanish control well into the nineteenth century. In fact, both countries were the last New World colonies retained by Spain. In order to keep control of the two islands, Spain granted them increasing autonomy and representation in the Spanish parliament. There was one uprising in 1868 in Puerto Rico, the *Grito de Lares*, but it was short-lived. One year before finally losing its colonies to the United States, Spain issued a Charter of Autonomy, which granted the island the right to self-government with its own political parties and elected officials. Self-government would not return to the island for nearly a century.

Puerto Rico's Un-holiday

On July 25, 1898, American troops landed on the island, lowered the Spanish flag, and forced Spain to surrender the island to the United States. Forty-four years later, on July 25, 1952, Governor Luis Muñoz proclaimed that the island was now the Commonwealth of Puerto Rico, and voters in the commonwealth responded by reelecting him by an overwhelming majority in their first general election under the new statute. So July 25 is celebrated as Constitution Day, but not as a day of independence for Puerto Rico. In fact, it would be best to disassociate the word "independence" from the island altogether.

Inhabited by more than three million people whose first language is Spanish, the island cannot be called a sovereign country or even a state. Ceded to the United States after the Spanish American War by the Treaty of Paris on December 10, 1898, Puerto Rico did not receive its commonwealth status from the United States until fifty-three years had passed and Puerto Ricans passed a referendum that gave them the right to draft their own constitution.

Independence still eludes the country, so July 25 in Puerto Rico is celebrated differently depending on the political leanings of the individual. For some, it's a day of protest against the island's commonwealth status and lack of independence. For others, it's a day of celebration and recognition of the symbiotic relationship between Puerto Rico and the United States.

NATIONAL PUERTO RICAN DAY

Celebration of Diversity in the City

WHEN **PUERTO RICO** became the property of the United States, the transition was far from painless. The island shared a language and culture with Spain, but it had little in common with the American way of doing things. For the first forty years, United States leaders approached the governance of Puerto Rico as an "Americanization" project. This was based largely on the belief that Puerto Ricans had to be assimilated into the language, culture, and values of the United States in order to be prepared for self-government. The imposition of

English as the only language of instruction was a dismal failure and had to be reversed by the 1940s.

The paternalistic policy employed toward the island by the United States was not well received by the people. The first concession made by the United States to appease islanders was the Jones Act in 1917. Signed by President Woodrow Wilson, the act granted U.S. citizenship to Puerto Ricans, but it also required them to serve in the Armed Forces, for which they were needed during World War I. Self-government expanded on the island with the Jones Act, which established a popularly elected Senate in Puerto Rico opposite the existing House of Representatives.

With the United States distracted by two world wars, Puerto Rican politics and doctrines began to emerge. The debate today centers on three possibilities: complete independence, statehood, or continued commonwealth status. Even though this debate may never be resolved, there will always be a strong connection between Puerto Rico and New York, and Puerto Ricans in the United States needed a festival to celebrate the culture and the island. The answer to this need was the National Puerto Rican Day parade.

Begun in New York City in 1957, the New York Puerto Rican Day Parade first extended over a few blocks in Manhattan. In 1995, it became the National Puerto Rican Day Parade, with the participation of national delegates, and now spans five miles and takes six hours to complete, becoming an impressive sea of red, white, and blue created by the millions of Puerto Rican flags held by the onlookers. The parade is usually held on the second Sunday in June. On the day of the parade, *nuyoricans* become the biggest

Traditional Tostones y Mojito

No Caribbean celebration experience is complete without sampling the tasty snack called *tostones*. The first thing revelers should know, especially those who are new to the dish, is that although the root element of the *tostone*, the plantain, is a cousin of the banana, *tostones* should not be confused with a similar dessert, the Chinese fried banana. The *tostone* is a salty snack that invariably is paired with a traditional garlic dip, called *mojito*. The following recipes are so simple and tasty that *tostones* will become a party favorite.

flag-wavers in the world. The Puerto Rican flag is everywhere: worn on T-shirts, painted on body parts, and attached to anything and everything.

At the time of the 1990 census, 3.8 million people were living on the island, and 2.6 million *nuyoricans* were living in New York. These numbers have grown in the past decade and the parade has a larger and larger attendance every year. It attracts people from other cultures as well. In 1999, two million people enjoyed the parade. Besides its 100 floats, vendors working the sidelines of the parade present for your enjoyment wonderful Puerto Rican delicacies like *arroz con gandules* (rice and chickpeas), *tostones* (fried plantains), and *pasteles*. The treats for the ear are also irresistible, especially *bomba* and *plena,* with a few *merengues* added in for more flavor.

Tostones (fried plantains)

3 green plantains
2 cups oil
salt (optional)

To prepare plantains for frying, peel and slice plantains into one-inch thick slices. Heat oil to 375 degrees. Don't allow oil to get so hot it smokes. Drop plantain slices into oil just long enough to brown. Watch carefully. With a slotted spoon, remove slices.

Using a wooden mallet or similar utensil, flatten the slices. Then refry them for another three to five minutes. Remove from oil, drain on paper towels, and salt to taste.

Mojito

4 garlic cloves
1 cup olive oil
dash salt

In a mortar and pestle, ground peeled garlic cloves. Transfer to a small bowl and add oil and salt. Mix well.

Refrigerate overnight and serve cold as a dip for *tostones.*

QUINCEAÑERAS, BIRTHDAYS, AND WEDDINGS

Life's Biggest Celebrations

Parties for Passages

IT'S ONLY human to mark life's different milestones with some kind of ceremony. To celebrate a birth or a marriage, or to honor a person's life once it ends are universal human needs. Ceremonies associated with life's passages do differ among cultures, and for Hispanics, the approach to life's important transitions, such as birthdays, coming of age, and marriage, involves certain distinctive customs.

It all begins with the birthday. To children, birthdays—like Christmas—seem magical. Parents go to extremes sometimes to plan birthday parties for their kids. In the United States, birthday parties require birthday cake, presents, and games, and Latinos add to these ingredients the ever-popular *piñata*. The origin of this party game may come as a surprise.

WHERE DID THE PIÑATA ORIGINATE?

Not used exclusively for birthdays in Mexico—there it's really more of a Christmas tradition—the *piñata* found its way into the United States through birthday celebrations. The origin of the papier-mâché vessel is unclear. Some writers trace it to the Aztecs, while others give it a European origin, beginning with the sixteenth century Italian treat-filled clay pots that were broken at parties and called *pignatta*. The European theory adds that *pignatta* appealed to the Spanish, who brought the custom to Latin America, where its popularity exploded.

The most significant birthday for girls, especially in Latino families, takes place at age fifteen. The idea of celebrating coming of age is not a new one. Societies worldwide mark the journey from adolescence into adulthood with marked rituals. Instead of a debut, Latinos put on a party called a *quinceañera*, but like a debut, the *quinceañera* is significant for the parents as well. The preparations of both the parents and the debutante for this celebration can rival most weddings.

Turning fifteen is not the only celebration of the journey through life. There are graduations and new jobs to toast. The next big celebration, however, is the wedding. For some couples, getting married may be one of the most important events in their lives, second only perhaps to becoming parents. Consequently, a wedding can present the chance to throw one of the biggest celebrations imaginable. Hispanic weddings can be quite extravagant, and they also call upon unique traditions during the ceremony and the reception.

Celebrating life involves recognizing the milestones that make everyone unique. Many Latino traditions, like the *piñata*, have already been incorporated into these festivities. There are still more life customs, from the *quinceañera* to the dollar dance at weddings, that hold their own particular appeal.

Happy Birthday, or Feliz Cumpleaños

Children eagerly anticipate birthdays, and these special celebrations are second only to Christmas in gift giving. Many customs have evolved around birthday celebrations, such as cake, candles, ice cream, and the singing of that difficult melody "Happy Birthday." The traditional Spanish birthday song, "Las Mañanitas" is a bit more melodic. Birthday parties across the United States can be extremely extravagant, with hired entertainment such as clowns or magicians. Parents may also opt to take the party out of the house and to a restaurant that caters to children's birthday parties.

Party games have changed as well. Pin the Tail on the Donkey used to be a birthday party staple, but it has been replaced by a Mexican party game, the *piñata*. The ground rules of both games are similar: children are given a simple task to perform but must do it blindfolded. The object of the *piñata* game is to break it open to get the candies inside. The *piñata* is usually suspended on a tree branch—this game should be played outside—with someone manipulating its position by pulling the rope up or down. The child is blindfolded and then spun around, gently, for added disorientation. It takes a while to break open the *piñata,* but once it rains down its treasure, children rush in to collect the treats.

Exactly when the *piñata* became a crossover hit in the United States isn't clear. "People used to think it was a Hispanic thing, a cultural thing. Now it's a party thing," says Party Star employee Jessica Vargas, in a September 22, 1994, article in the *Los Angeles Sentinel*. Party Star is an Anaheim, California–based company and one of the largest suppliers of *piñatas* in the United States. It is owned by three siblings, all natives of Costa Rica: Juan and Oscar Vargas and Aurora Dixon. Dixon started making *piñatas* out of her garage for her own children's parties. Once the neighbors saw them, everyone wanted them. As the demand for her *piñatas* increased, her brother Oscar convinced her to open a shop.

In her book *Mexican Crafts and Craftspeople* (Associated University Presses: Cranbury, New Jersey, 1987) author Marian Harvey argues that the *piñata* may have an Italian, Aztec, or Spanish heritage, but the most fervent promoters of the party *piñata* were the Spaniards.

Although it's recognized as a children's game, Harvey says that the piñata was originally for adults. In Spanish colonial days, the *piñata* was filled with jewels rather than candy and broken by men and women rather than children. Harvey asserts that the root of the word itself is Spanish, not Italian as it would seem, beginning with the word *apinar,* which means to cluster, and *piña,* which means cluster of flowers or fruit. Says Harvey: "Neither the *piñata*, nor anything like it, is known to have existed in Mexico before the Conquest. Paper, as we know it, was brought by the Spanish, which makes one believe the *piñata*, too, was brought from Spain."

Piñatas do exist all over Latin America, but the papier-mâché versions were designed in Mexico. Today, Tijuana, Mexico is considered the *piñata* capital of the world.

GIRL POWER

It is a celebration that reminds everyone of the bright promise of a girl's future. It acknowledges her early successes and lets her know that she is special and that she is loved. What could be so affirming? The Latino coming-of-age party for girls, called the *quinceañera*. The name derives from the words for "fifteen" and "year" in Spanish, which are *quince* and *año*. The word is used for both the event and the debutante herself. It has also been called *la fiesta rosada* (pink party) because the color pink symbolizes the young girl who has blossomed into a woman.

The *quinceañera* is one of the few universal Latino holidays. Mexican Americans, Puerto Ricans, and Cuban Americans all celebrate the *quinceañera*, and in much the same fashion as it was celebrated by the ancients. Families still prepare for months for the celebration, which is marked by a spiritual as well as a social element.

Sweet Fifteen—La Quinceañera

The need to recognize the transition between childhood and adulthood is universal. Civilizations over the centuries have established rites of passage for both boys and girls. For young women in the United States, that event is often marked at age sixteen with Sweet Sixteen parties or debuts. This practice was promoted in the South in the nineteenth century with the debutante ball. A similar event is the Jewish coming of age at thirteen with the bas mitzvah for boys and the bat mitzvah for girls.

Coming-out parties were thought to have reached the New World during the French occupation of Mexico in the nineteenth century, but the *quinceañera's* roots go much deeper than that. In her book *Quinceañera* (Henry Holt and Company: New York, 1997) author Michele Salcedo explains, "The beginnings [of the *quinceañera*] go much further back, thousands of years back, to the indigenous people of our respective cultures. The Tainos and Arawaks, the Quechua and Toltecs, the Aztecs and Mayas, to name but a few—

all had rites of passage to mark the point in a child's life when she was a child no longer, but ready to make her contribution to society as an adult."

According to Mark Francis and Arturo J. Perez-Rodriguez in the book *Primero Dios: Hispanic Liturgical Resource* (Liturgy Training Publications: Chicago, 1997), both boys and girls initially participated in these rites of passage but only the celebration for girls has survived. As part of the preparation, girls were separated at age fifteen from their playmates and instead instructed on their importance to the community and their future roles as wives and mothers. "During the rite in its origins, the gods were thanked for the lives of these future mothers, and the young women pledged to fulfill their roles of service to the community," write the authors. "The *quinceañera* was gradually Christianized by the missionaries to highlight a personal affirmation of faith by the young woman and her willingness to become a good Christian wife and mother. It then became common to celebrate it in church, although apart from a Mass."

Unlike many Latino traditions, however, the *quinceañera* tends to be cross-denominational and not exclusively Catholic. The social significance of the *quinceañera* may be what most attracts attention. It bears a great similarity to many weddings, except in this case the "bride" wears pink. The pink color symbolizes the girl's coming of age, but the preferred emphasis is on the girl's maturity rather than on her sexuality. In many *quinceañeras*, the event begins with a Mass, but this is not always the case. Because of the event's great cost to the parents—an average of $10,000—some churches discourage their members from adopting the tradition. To offset the costs, families sometimes enlist the support of *padrinos* (sponsors) to cover particular items, from the dress to the cost of a band for the reception. This practice is also carried over to weddings.

The *quinceañera* chooses several of her friends to be her attendants, called the Court of Honor. These girls—there are usually fourteen of them to represent the debutante's previous years—start the procession, accompanied by their escorts. The parents usually enter the procession next, before their daughter. The *quinceañera* can have an escort, usually a brother, cousin, or friend, but some choose to have their parents as escorts instead.

There are interesting twists to the celebration as well. According to Salcedo, most Cuban families forgo the church service, while Mexican American families will almost always include it. The service can be a simple prayer or blessing from the priest, or a full Mass. Puerto Ricans will also generally opt for the Mass, which culminates with the mother of the *quinceañera* placing a tiara on her daughter's head and her father replacing her flats with high heels.

Despite the ceremony's high cost, many parents see *quinceañera* celebrations as a good investment. It reinforces the fact that their daughter is expected to take on more responsibility, and that symbolism does not escape the *quinceañera*. "Not to brag, but my daughter is unique in a lot of ways," says Mary Mendez, the mother of Brandy, who celebrated her *quinceañera* in 1994. Brandy's *quinceañera* was featured in a June 15–21 article in the *New Times* of Phoenix, Arizona. "I think it [the *quinceañera*] is good. Half of what's wrong with kids nowadays is they don't think about their future."

Bodas—Weddings with Latino Details

A lifetime is marked by transitions. Most are so small they're not noticed, but for the larger, more momentous steps, rituals and customs have evolved to mark those occasions. For many, marriage is certainly among the top three life changes. In the past, marriage meant that two individuals would leave their parents' home and build a life together. Today, more couples have already established themselves in careers and may have already started living together. But the significance of publicly declaring a lifetime commitment to one person is still great. Consequently, getting married is still surrounded by numerous traditions, beginning with the simple question, "Will you marry me?"

Besides the ceremony itself, many wedding traditions evolved out of superstition, with the intention of bringing luck to the newlyweds. Today, many superstitions remain, such as the groom not seeing the bride before the wedding or throwing rice to symbolize fertility. Other traditions evolved because they symbolized something that complemented the belief in the sacredness of marriage. The wedding ring dates back to antiquity, but it still exists today as an integral part of the wedding ceremony because its shape symbolizes the union of two people and the hope for never-ending love.

Latino weddings reflect the religious faith of the couple. The Catholic ceremony is pretty much the same as other Catholic ceremonies. But Latinos do add some unique touches, beginning with the Spanish word for wedding, which is *boda*. During a Latino wedding ceremony, onlookers may notice three additional components: the *arras* (coins), the *lazo* (yoke), and the *mantilla* (veil).

The National Institute of Hispanic Liturgy researched the marriage traditions and customs of Latinos and published its findings in *Gift and Promise Customs and Traditions in Hispanic Rites of Marriage* (Oregon Catholic Press: Portland, 1997). The book confirms that while many Latino customs such as the *arras* were introduced by the Spaniards, they also have roots in an ancient Iberian rite called the Mozarabic Rite, which refers to rituals celebrated by the Moors around A.D. 415–711. The Mozarabic Rite was suppressed by Pope Gregory VII in A.D. 1080 and was not reestablished until 1988, after the Vatican Council II. Therefore, like many customs, the *arras* began as a social custom before becoming part of the "sacramental" celebration.

In the old rite, the *arras* may have been the predecessor to the exchange of marriage rings—it was from this rite that the wedding rings eventually emerged. There were four phases in the Mozarabic marriage rite: the bedchamber blessing, the celebration of vespers, the *arras* (marriage tokens) blessing, and the couple blessing. The name *arras* comes from the Latin phrase for the actual exchange of vows, which was *ordo arrarum* (order of pledges). In the ceremony, a ring or pledge token was exchanged between the bride and groom. The pledge between the man and woman was sealed with this exchange. According to the book, "Although it is not clear what exactly was given as a token during the first millennium, the *arras* today is a small cask containing thirteen gilded or plated coins in the smallest size or denomination; the baker's dozen symbolizes prosperity." Although rings replaced the *arras* as the token of exchange, in today's Latino ceremonies, both rings and *arras* are blessed and exchanged after the marriage vows are given.

Evidence of the first *lazo* also dates back to antiquity. One of the sources cited by the National Institute of Hispanic Liturgy is Isidore of Seville, who wrote *De Ecclesiasticis Officiis* in the seventh century. In this book, the author established in writing the organization of the Spanish Church. According to Isadore of Seville, during the marriage ceremony, the couple wore a *vitta*, or garland. The *vitta* was white and purple, symbolizing purity and procreation. The couple wore it over their shoulders. Centuries later an actual yoke was placed across the bride and groom, linking the pair together during the nuptial blessing.

There is also an indigenous root for the *lazo*. In Meso-American ceremonies, the couple sat on separate mats but when the vows or official union was proclaimed, the tassels of the mats were tied, signaling the union. Later, the Aztecs actually tied the mantle of the groom to the bride's dress as a sign of marriage. Today the *lazo* is much more ornate. It is usually beaded with faux pearls, with two loops to go over the shoulders of the bride and groom. The *lazo* can also be a double-looped rosary with the cross hanging at the middle, and some *lazos* have even been made of fresh flowers.

Another ancient custom that has crossed over into all wedding ceremonies is the veil, or *mantilla*. In the old ritual, the bride offered her hand to the celebrant (priest) after exchanging vows. The priest then offered the couple the blessing of the newly married. They were covered with a veil, the bride completely and the groom only over his shoulders. At the end of the blessing, the bride's hand was offered to the groom. The use of the veil is ancient, says the Institute: "Roman brides were covered completely by a red veil, the *flam-*

meum, which served as a symbol of purity and protection against evil spirits. This surely influenced the Spanish custom."

Today the veil is worn by the bride more as a symbol of virginity when she enters the church. The original intention of the custom reappears in Latino ceremonies when the *lazo* is used to hold part of the bride's veil over the groom's shoulder. Other Latino ceremonies use a separate *mantilla* in place of a *lazo* during the ceremony—rather than the bride's veil—to put over the shoulders of the bride and groom.

There are many other components to the ceremony, including cushions for the bride and groom and a rosary. For Puerto Rican brides, the orange blossom is an essential flower, and Cuban men follow the Spanish tradition of wearing the wedding ring on their right ring finger rather than the left. Each element does carry a certain cost, so Latinos enlist the support of family members and friends—as they do with quinceañera and ask them to take on the role of *padrinos* (sponsors). Although the literal translation for *padrinos* is godparents, several *padrinos* can participate in a wedding by purchasing different items, from the *lazo* to the band that plays at the reception. The *padrinos'* support is usually listed on the wedding invitation.

At the wedding reception, more customs emerge. Latino weddings must include a dance where traditional music is played, and some add the "dollar dance," in which guests line up to buy a dance with the bride or

Simple Ball Piñata

To make this colored ball piñata, you will need the following supplies:

1 large balloon
Several sheets of brightly colored tissue paper
Newspapers
Water and flour to make paste

Other shapes can be added to the round ball *piñata*, but the ball formed by the balloon will be the core. It provides the receptacle for the candy and prizes.

The basic material of modern *piñatas* is papier-mâché. Inflate a round balloon as large as it will go. Cut up strips of newspaper. Mix the flour and water (one part flour to two parts water) to create the glue paste. Soak the newspaper strips one at a time in the paste, then layer them over the balloon. This is the basic papier-mâché technique.

Continue layering the paste-soaked strips of newspaper around the balloon until it is completely covered. Don't layer the paper around the balloon tie; instead, keep the tie exposed and create a small hole. This opening will be where the piñata is filled with candy. Let each papier-mâché layer dry. Apply at least six layers.

After the papier-mâché is dry, take the tissue paper and cut it into two-inch-wide strips that are of different lengths. The strips should be long enough to wrap around the papier-mâché ball. Cut one edge of the strips to create a fringe, and curl the fringe by wrapping it around a cylindrical object. For super-curly curls use a pen or pencil. Glue each strip, one by one, to the ball. You could paint the papier-mâché to cover the newspaper print, or simply layer the curled strips closely so that the paper print is obscured. Create a pattern of color with the tissue paper.

After the balloon is covered with colored tissue paper, pop the balloon. Insert candy, confetti, and prizes in the circular opening where the balloon tie-off used to be. Attach a piece of wood or wire across this opening, which will be used to help suspend the piñata. Close the opening with tape and camouflage the closure with tissue paper. Then, let the games begin!

groom. The couple usually takes the proceeds on the honeymoon. Souvenirs of the wedding are placed at the tables for each guest, from chocolates to knickknacks. Another tradition is called the *capia*, which is a ribbon with the names of the bride and groom printed on it, worn by each guest.

Not all Latinos subscribe to every traditional element for their weddings. Many couples today tend to pick and choose among them. When planning their wedding, Rochelle Herrera and Gustavo Gonzalez discussed the traditional elements like the *lazo*, the cushions, and the *arras,* and of them all, chose only the *arras* to be incorporated into the ceremony. As young professionals, Rochelle and Gus didn't feel the need to incorporate the *padrino* tradition of sponsoring. They preferred to keep it simple and not obligate relatives to help pay for the wedding. The *arras,* however, were important to the bride. "My mother had been saving the *arras*—thirteen silver dimes—since I was a little girl. She considers them a sort of dowry. She had some for my sister's wedding, and she even has some saved for my brother," says Herrera. "I also liked the sentiment since I was presenting them to Gus instead of him presenting them to me, and it seemed to say, "What's yours is mine, and what's mine is yours.'"

Whatever choices Latinos make, from the *piñata* at birthday parties, to *quinceañeras*, to wedding traditions like the *lazo* and *arras*, these rituals help point the way forward in life, while focusing on the joys of the present. *¡Felicidades!*

FALL

Ancestors and Homeland

~

SEPTEMBER 16
DIEZ Y SEIS

~

SEPTEMBER 8 AND NOVEMBER 19
FEAST DAYS OF THE CARIBBEAN VIRGINS

~

OCTOBER 12
DÍA DE LA RAZA

~

NOVEMBER 2
DÍA DE LOS MUERTOS

OTOÑO

FALL BRINGS cooler weather and a time for reflection and remembrance. Coincidence or not, many Latino holidays that appear in the autumn hark back to an earlier history and to indigenous ancestry. Many of the fall holidays deal with history and homeland.

On Diez y Seis (September 16), the anniversary of Mexico's freedom from Spanish rule, Mexicans celebrate their Independence Day while Mexican Americans fuel their longings and pride for their motherland. In the United States, Diez y Seis has turned into a huge celebration in cities across the nation.

In September and November two important feast days honoring prominent versions of the Virgin Mary allow Latinos to celebrate their religious and cultural ties. Cubans honor their patroness, Nuestra Señora de la Caridad del Cobre (Our Lady of Charity of El Cobre) on September 8, and Puerto Ricans combine the celebration of the island's discovery with tribute to Nuestra Señora de la Divina Providencia (Our Lady of Divine Providence) on November 19.

Other important fall holidays are Día de la Raza on October 12 and Día de los Muertos on November 2, times to commemorate the "race" and the dead, respectively. Día de la Raza presents an interesting cultural reaction to—some would say rejection of—Columbus Day. And Día de los Muertos, or the Day of the Dead, shows Latinos' most unique approach to death. Although its roots are strictly Mexican, this ritual continues to find new celebrants in all Latino communities and its practice has become a form of art.

DIEZ Y SEIS

A Triumph over Tyranny

CONTRARY TO popular belief, Cinco de Mayo is not Mexico's Independence Day holiday—September 16 (*diez y seis de septiembre*) is. The date of September 16 does not mark the day when the war for independence ended but instead the day it began. More and more Mexican American communities in the United States have organized fiestas to celebrate Mexican independence, and though they tend to have the same trappings as most Cinco de Mayo celebrations, the symbolic impact of this date is much different.

THE GRITO

The *grito de dolores* appeals on several levels and has multiple meanings. *Grito* means to cry out, and *dolores* means sadness as well as the town in Mexico where Father Miguel Hidalgo y Costilla rang the bells and cried for Mexico's freedom. Mexico's cry for independence is alive and well today, as it is included between the refrains of many a *corrido* sung by traditional Mexican musicians.

Sometimes these *gritos* are long and involved, arching over octaves and sending a chill down the spine. The common shout, "*¡Ay, Ay, Ay!*" comes from a cry of pain over the poor living conditions of Mexico's masses, issued by Father Hidalgo. This cry, or *grito*, signaled the beginning of the war for independence from Spain. That's why the *grito* always has and always will emphasize the continuing struggle for justice. *¡Viva la revolución!*

Just as fireworks, picnics, and the colors red, white, and blue are associated with July 4—the United States' Independence Day—the customs associated with the celebrations on September 16 have symbolic importance. These customs include the colors of the Mexican flag (red, white, and green), the *grito*, *mariachi* and *conjunto* music, *ballet folklórico*, and culinary staples like *gorditas* and *tamales*. With its political and historical significance, this holiday offers participants some insight into the events that molded the cultural psyche of Mexico.

Mexico's Progress Toward Independence

In the early seventeenth century, Mexico had settled into a somewhat stable colonial situation. The country's riches kept Spain, more specifically the Spanish Crown, satiated. The other major authority was the Catholic Church, which influenced the poor as well as the upper classes. The country in effect was controlled by two powers, but they were not equal. The Church had more influence, but as long as the flow of gold, silver, and chocolate remained uninterrupted, Spain was satisfied to let the Church attend to the business of the people, and the priests happily complied. They collected tithes to support the Church but also provided lenient loans to landowners and entrepreneurs. Writes Enrique Krauze, author of *Mexico: Biography of Power* (Harper Collins: New York, 1997): "Ever since the spiritual conquest, the priests of Mexico held much greater and more direct power than any that might be imposed by Spain or for that matter Rome. They could count on the zealous loyalty and devotion of the people."

By the eighteenth century, the tables began to turn, and the Spanish Crown sought to take control back from the Church. It followed Spain's involvement in the Seven Years' War (1756–1763) when Charles III ordered the priests expelled from Mexico. Many converted natives opposed this treatment of the priests, even to the point of armed rebellion. The Crown responded with even harsher treatment of the natives, including a massive slaughter. On top of this, Spain coopted the process of collecting tithes. "The expulsion of the Jesuits was, at least in one respect, a costly mistake for the Bourbons," writes Krauze. "It generated a new spirit of Mexican patriotism that fed on the longstanding resentments of the Creoles."

There were many turning points that converged to bring "New Spain" [Mexico] toward a revolution from its colonial master. Two revolutions had already occurred—the American Revolution and the French Revolution—and the concepts of liberty and democracy for which these revolutions were fought did not go unnoticed by the Spanish missionaries or the Mexican intellectuals. They could not ignore the poor living conditions imposed by the Spanish Crown on their parishioners. Ironically, it would be the Church, which had partnered with Spain to conquer Mexico, Latin America, and certain islands in the Caribbean, that would produce vital leaders to bring on Mexico's fight for freedom.

Another factor was the crippling debt Spain had begun to accrue in skirmish after skirmish with its two strongest enemies, England and France. The country looked to its wealthy colony, New Spain, the Spanish nationals still living there (*gachupines*), the landowners (*criollos*), and the remaining masses, to pay for its war debt. Spain crossed the line with the Church when it took over all rights to collect debt owed to the Church, which had begun to issue financial assistance to landowners in New Spain. The Church was a much less rigorous lender than Spain intended to be. Under the Church, loans had been extended and affordable payment schedules arranged, but the Crown changed that. "Suddenly—through the stroke of a royal pen—the Bourbon Crown created its right to demand the immediate payment of all these debts in full, offering nothing but a voucher (*vale*) in return—a promise of compensation in some uncertain future," writes Krauze. Naturally, there was an immediate protest, and although some priests tried to influence the monarchy in Spain to reverse its decisions in order to maintain control of Mexico, other priests, one in particular, who was a native *criollo*, took this opportunity to take Mexico one step closer to independence.

Mexico's Cry for Independence

Political revolutions are rarely peaceful, and the war for Mexico's independence from Spain was no exception. It would take eleven years to finish and would leave Mexico economically devastated, spiritually depleted, and ripe for one last invasion from France. Although he would not live to see the success of what he started, Father Miguel Hidalgo y Costilla remained a driving force of the revolution that he set in motion with a yell on the fateful day of September 16, 1810, in the small town of Dolores in the state of Guanajuato, Mexico.

Hidalgo could be described as unconventional, but that would be an understatement. An ordained Catholic priest, he was a recognized theologian and a natural rebel. In his view, Church doctrine was continually up for interpretation, as were his duties as a priest. As a landowner, the green-eyed and fair-haired Hidalgo hailed from an old family of *criollos* (Spaniards born in Mexico) and his vows of chastity and poverty proved a constant challenge. There had been efforts to excommunicate him (eventually a close colleague succeeded) based on evidence of gambling, womanizing, and a casual approach to the Church's teachings. An individualist, he encouraged his congregation to study the Bible "with the freedom of mind to discuss what we want without fearing the Inquisition."

But Hidalgo had a greater love than his love of the Church—his love of Mexico and its people. A revolution needs this type of charismatic leader and Hidalgo did not fail his country. "Hidalgo was not only a restless priest but an eccentric one, a free and brilliant man, who attracted—and seduced—the most enlightened of his contemporaries but unsettled the more rigid and conservative. They vaguely sensed in him the seed of something new and disconcerting," writes Krauze.

Mexico had been ruled by Spain for 400 years. During that time, Spain had enforced a caste system that favored a small group of landowners over the peasant population, made up in large part of descendants of Mexico's original inhabitants. Reaching far beyond this secular control was the pervasive influence of the Catholic Church, which would continue to influence Mexican politics even after Mexico achieved independence from Spain. Highly intelligent and well read, and angered by the poverty he observed in his parish, Hidalgo was destined to take the lead in the revolution. But one event would provide the catalyst for him to take a stand.

In 1804, the Spanish Crown required all landowners to make exorbitant payments under the threat of auctioning off their land. Hacienda owners like Hidalgo's family came close to bankruptcy, and closer to home, Hidalgo's younger brother, Manuel, supposedly went mad and died within a few years from the pressure. Hidalgo would forever hold the Crown responsible for his family's loss.

An individualist rather than a military man, Hidalgo's ideas about revolution were anarchistic. Rather than upholding revolution as part of a democratic process, he employed the mob rule approach to war, urging his native Indian parishioners to take up any kind of weapon, from guns to rocks, and turn out the Spanish. On the *diez y seis de septiembre,* Hidalgo rang the cathedral bell to summon his flock into the church square and inflamed the group with this order: "Death to the Spaniards! Long live the Virgen de Guadalupe!" According to Krauze there is not a consensus as to Hidalgo's real words. Says Krauze: "We know he called on the Indians to open the jails of Dolores, free the prisoners, and lock up the Spaniards, and that he authorized the sacking of houses and haciendas belonging to the Spanish-born (*gapuchines*) and allowed his followers to kill and satisfy their instincts for revenge."

Bloody battles followed Hidalgo's *grito,* or cry for freedom. Krauze writes about the massacre at Guanajuato where, despite shutting themselves up in a granary, many Creole and Spanish men were slaughtered by Hidalgo's forces: "As if history were taking an atrocious revenge for the massacres of Indians by the conquistadors at Cholula and the great temple of Tenochtitlán, Indians and castes (descendants from black slaves) from the city joined Hidalgo's Indian brigades in slaughtering all the Spanish men." Hidalgo had instilled in his followers the desire to revolt, and with his own personal issues against the Spanish rule, he became torn as to whether to quell his followers' growing blood lust or to continue to lead them.

Writes Krauze: "Hidalgo would later confess that he knew of no way to ignite the war other than the one he put into effect: using the prestige of his priesthood to appeal to the elemental passions of his Indian parishioners, among them plunder and revenge. . . . He wanted to destroy the old order, to cure its social and ethnic injustices, to avenge the old grievances of the Creoles and to avenge Manuel, the brother who had died. He wanted a universal conflagration."

Hidalgo may have started the revolution, but he could not keep it going. Lacking in military training, Hidalgo led his followers (at one point 80,000 strong), to a standoff in Mexico City, says Krauze, "armed with lances, stones, and sticks and so ready to plunder Mexico City that they had brought sacks with them for carrying off what they would seize." Although many believe he could have ended the war there and defeated the Spanish army, the priest instead withdrew. He may have tired of the carnage and opted for a more diplomatic resolution. He retreated to Guadalajara, where he outlined two important goals for the revolution—to abolish taxes and to return the land to its original owners, the Indians. He was arrested and executed in the city of Chihuahua less than a year from the start of the war, July 30, 1811.

Another priest, José María Morelos y Pavón, had heard Hidalgo's cry for freedom and taken on his cause. Unlike Hidalgo, Morelos was of mixed Spanish and Indian ancestry—a *mestizo*—and hailed from much more humble beginnings. Hidalgo and Morelos met shortly after the former first took up arms, and the forty-year-old Morelos accepted the responsibility of organizing the rebellion in the south. Unlike Hidalgo, Morelos studied his military textbooks and led a more organized rebellion. Hidalgo's role in gaining Mexico's independence has been more lionized, but it was Morelos who led the revolution's major battles.

Like Hidalgo, Morelos would not see the end of the struggle. He was executed in 1815. Unlike Hidalgo, Morelos would have more of an imprint on the terms of Mexico's freedom; he actually helped draft the country's first constitution. In this constitution, Morelos effectively captured the concepts of democracy and incorporated them into Mexico's social and cultural makeup. Writes Krauze: "Morelos did not see the struggle for independence as merely a matter of arms and politics. . . . Morelos had become conscious of the social inequality between the impoverished, dark-skinned Mexico of the Indians and castes and the affluent, white Mexico of the Spaniards and Creoles. Out of these memories he drew his ideology . . . an invitation to reach out and build an agreement, pointing toward the future." Mexico finally won its independence in 1821.

Mexican Independence Celebrations in the U.S.

Like Cinco de Mayo, celebrations marking the *dies y seis de septiembre* in the United States probably date back to when the Southwest was still part of Mexico. But the trend has grown in recent years, to some extent as a backlash against Cinco de Mayo and the misperception that that holiday celebrates Mexican independence. Parents and teachers felt the need to clarify that September 16 is the Mexican Fourth of July.

Throughout the southwestern United States, Latino organizations continue to emerge as sponsors of Diez y Seis celebrations. One of the oldest events takes place in Dallas at Pike Park in the heart of the Latino barrio called Little Mexico. Since 1965, the Federation of Mexican Organizations has sponsored the event, not only to reinforce cultural pride in the community but also as a means of educating the entire Dallas community about the history of its Latinos. Catalina Valdez Scott has helped organize the event for several years and has seen more and more interest develop in the entire Dallas community. "We've been getting calls from people who aren't Hispanic . . . all wanting information," she said in a *Dallas Morning News* article. "We want people of Mexican descent to feel proud of their heritage and the history of Mexico. People are proud of who they are, other people are appreciating that, and that makes me happy."

Like all cultural festivals, food, music, and dance are the three main ingredients for making Diez y Seis a success. In Texas, the traditional dishes like *tacos*, *gorditas*, *tamales* and *fajitas* are the usual fare, along with American festival staples like hamburgers and hot dogs. The vendors tend to be community or neighborhood groups hoping to raise funds for their nonprofit organizations. Desserts like *raspadas* (similar to snow cones but with fresh fruit syrups) and *buñuelos* are also common, in addition to ice cream and cotton candy.

The music will begin with *mariachis,* the familiar singing troupes of eight to ten members, dressed as stylized *charros* (cowboys), and playing the trumpet, violin, guitar, and *bajo sexto* (six-string bass). Although many assume that *mariachi* music is traditional Mexican music, it was only embraced by Mexico; its origin is actually French. But the style and costumes of the players are uniquely Mexican. Often, local *ballet folklórico* troupes will be invited to participate in the event as well, dancing to the *mariachi* music. Later in the day, most celebrations feature a full-scale concert with bands playing a variety of styles of Mexican music from *conjunto* to *tejano,* and culminating with the most popular band in the genre that the sponsoring organization can afford.

Salsa for All Occasions

The flavor of Mexico has been the most successful ambassador for this culture. The problem comes when people separate the flavor from the nation. Joining a Diez y Seis celebration will help reinforce that link. Since salsa now ranks as the number-one condiment in this country, surpassing ketchup, a simple way to keep the spirit of Diez y Seis is to make homemade salsa. It's quick, easy, affordable, and delicious.

Hot Salsa

4 medium tomatoes (avoid romas or sweet tomatoes)
½ large onion
1 handful of cilantro leaves, stems trimmed off
4 jalapeños
1 teaspoon salt
¼ cup tomato sauce
2 tablespoons lime juice

In a blender, mix onion, tomatoes, jalapeños, and cilantro leaves. For a

Since Diez y Seis is celebrated from coast to coast, you might even hear *salsa* or *merengue* at one of the celebrations.

Activities usually begin in the morning with special events targeted toward children, but on the first day of what tends to be a three-day event, there is a required action that signals the beginning of the celebration—the *grito de dolores*. Usually prominent Latino civic leaders are asked to perform this ritual and some festivals may continue with a *grito* contest.

Most American cities with sizable Mexican American populations participate in this holiday, even northern cities like Philadelphia, Pennsylvania. Slightly more than five percent of a population doesn't seem like a lot, but in a city the size of Philadelphia, that number translates into 89,000 people of Hispanic heritage. The bulk of that group is Puerto Rican, but a growing Mexican and Mexican American population has joined the migrant workers in the area's outlying mushroom fields. There's even a Mexican consulate in Philadelphia, and eight years ago the consul at the time, Patricia Soria, decided it was time to expand Mexican cultural festivals beyond Cinco de Mayo and recognize Mexican independence in Philadelphia. "It all started with the Associación de México, which was founded by our consul at the time, Patricia Soria, who decided to hold a small celebration for the local Mexican community," explains Elena Riley, director of the Mexican Cultural Center in Philadelphia. "It continued to grow, and two years later, the Mexican government founded the Mexican Cultural Center to take it over."

Although the center does recognize Cinco de Mayo ("We're forced to," says Riley), it's more of a subdued event and is heavy on the educational side. The Diez y Seis celebration, on the other hand, is the center's main event, featuring the usual components, the *grito* (performed by the consul), Mexican food (tacos, *carnitas, tostadas,* and Mexican beer), and music and dancing. "For the Diez y Seis, the music and dancing is all Mexican folk, from *mariachis, boleros,* and *conjunto.* We also bring in *ballet folklórico* dancers from Puebla or Oaxaca, Mexico," says Riley.

This Diez y Seis celebration has expanded to three locations in Philadelphia. The main one is at Penn's Landing, an outside arena that attracts 25,000 to 30,000 people, but there are two smaller events in outlying counties. The center and the city's migrant education program rent buses to bring the migrant workers to these events. In Philadelphia, the event attracts a large crowd. "We try to show the best of Mexican culture and tradition," Riley stresses.

With any cultural festival, culture is the main attraction. Diez y Seis may have a much different history than Cinco de Mayo, but both celebrations affirm the spirit of a people who fought for freedom from a country that destroyed one culture while creating a new one.

chunky consistency, use the chop setting on the blender for the onions and jalapeños and blend the rest in for no more than one minute. Pour mixture into a saucepan and begin to boil. Add salt and lime juice to taste. Boil for about five minutes. After salsa cools, place in glass jars. A recycled store-bought salsa jar works fine. Store in refrigerator. Boiling and refrigerating will help the salsa last for as long as one month.

Note: This is a hot salsa recipe. Boiling will take some of the heat from the peppers, but for weaker tastebuds, one jalapeño may be enough. For stronger palates, simply add more jalapeños.

Caribbean
Virgins

THE WORSHIP OF MARY

Marian ideology—the veneration of Mary as a separate religious icon—has been accepted and promoted by the Catholic Church for centuries. It was used very effectively in the conversion of the Americas because the native people found it easier to make the switch from goddess as Earth mother to Mary, the mother of God. Most Latin American cultures have a Virgin who speaks to them, sometimes in the form of an apparition but always spiritually.

The Catholic conversion in the Americas was so complete that every country on the continent boasts its own patroness. In the United States, the patron Virgin is Our Lady of the Immaculate Conception. Many communities within the Catholic faith have been lucky enough to claim a visitation by the Virgin Mary, and in so doing, adopt their own patroness

Virgin. From Argentina's Nuestra Señora de Luján (Our Lady of Luján) to Venezuela's Nuestra Señora de Coromoto (Our Lady of Coromoto), to Cuba's Nuestra Señora de la Caridad del Cobre (Our Lady of Charity of El Cobre), to Puerto Rico's Nuestra Señora de la Divina Providencia (Our Lady of the Divine Inspiration), there is a Virgin for everyone. Our Lady of Guadalupe has been named Patroness of the Americas because she is the only Virgin to have made an apparition on this continent.

Unique to the Catholic faith is the concept of "Mary worship." Unlike the image of many indigenous goddesses who could be nurturing and brutal, Mary, the mother of God, is appealing because of her gentleness. She does not judge or condemn. She appears to the weak or downtrodden with a message of hope and love. The more compelling and enduring Virgin Mary stories usually incorporate a political as well as a spiritual tone. The Virgin of Guadalupe appeared to an Indian and spoke to him in his native language. For this, and because her image reflected the mixed races of Mexico, Latino devotion to her is unwavering. In the role of a patroness, the Virgin Mary has unfathomable power, and the patronesses of Cuba and Puerto Rico, Our Lady of Charity of El

Cobre and Our Lady of the Divine Inspiration, respectively, have had a similar impact on believers from those islands. Cubans mark the feast day of Nuestra Señora de la Caridad de Cobre on September 8 and Puerto Ricans pay homage to Nuestra Señora de la Divina Providencia on November 19.

The Cuban patron saint, La Virgen de Cobre, has many legends. The central theme, however, follows that of most religious sightings: she appeared to the downtrodden in their most desperate hour and gave them the strength to overcome adversity. In one version of the story, the poor are copper miners who were told to fish to feed the other workers. They cast their nets and instead caught a copper statuette of the Virgin Mary. The shrine to the Virgin was built in Santiago, Cuba, and is the site of a pilgrimage performed by Cubans each September 8. Cuban exiles felt the loss of their Virgin so acutely that they built a replica of the shrine and installed it in Miami.

In Puerto Rico, Our Lady of the Divine Providence was not native to the island—her legend began in Italy. Her devotion found worshipers in Catalonia, Spain, and a Spaniard, Bishop Gil Esteve Tomás, inevitably transported her to the New World. Inspired by this patroness, the bishop rallied the local townspeople to help rebuild a church in her honor that included a beautifully sculpted wooden image of her. It is taken from an original oil painting and depicts the Virgin with the Baby Jesus on her lap while she lovingly watches over him.

In his thesis, "The Blessed Virgin Mary, Mother of the Divine Providence Puerto Rico," Father Michael Meléndez clarifies that "Marian devotions are not set upon pagan worship, contrary to popular fundamentalist beliefs . . . but [are] rather a moment in which the Christian is called to reflect on the life of Mary in terms of her relationship to Christ, salvation, and the Church."

Most patron Virgins earn their distinction because their legends, perpetuated through an apparition or another miraculous event, take place in that country. Although there was another Virgin of Guadalupe in Spain, the Virgin of Guadalupe became the patroness of Mexico because of her appearance in that country and the miraculous *tilma* that bears her likeness. The same is true of Cuba's patron Virgin, Our Lady of Charity, who also shares a name with a Spanish Virgin but is inextricably linked with the island because of the small statuette of her that was found there by three slaves. The patroness of Puerto Rico, Our Lady of the Divine Providence, wasn't sighted on the island, but for the many Puerto Ricans who revere her, that's just a technicality. Like all patron Virgins, Puerto Rico's provides the inspiration and comfort that comes naturally from the mother of God.

FEAST DAY OF NUESTRA SEÑORA DE LA DIVINA PROVIDENCIA

Veneration of a Caribbean Virgin

THE STORY of Our Lady of the Divine Providence begins in the thirteenth century, when she was venerated in the city of Arezzo, Tuscany, in Italy. Inspired by the work of Saint Francis of Assisi, seven wealthy merchants in the area embraced a vow of poverty and joined the order of the Servants of Mary. So devout were they that they left their daily sustenance up to the will of God. Saint Philip Benicio, who was the fifth superior of the order of the Servants of Mary, visited the friars one day. "Saint Philip Benicio found the friars to be completely confident in the Divine Providence because the [sic] asked for nothing from anyone. They trusted in a bountiful God who would provide for all their needs," writes Meléndez. After praying to the Virgin Mary to help the friars, Saint Philip discovered food at the door of the convent—two baskets full—but not a trace of how it got there. "Since that time, she was invoked as the Virgin of the Divine Providence."

Eventually, the devotion to this Virgin spread to Spain, where a shrine was built in Tarragona, Catalonia. A native of this region, Don Gil Esteve Tomás, was named bishop of Puerto Rico. He brought the devotion of this Virgin with him. When Tomás arrived on the island around the mid-nineteenth century, the thirty-third bishop of Puerto Rico found the cathedral in San Juan practically in ruins. He asked the Virgin for help, and although there was no apparition or other discovery, the church was restored by his parishioners in less than five years.

Once he had established devotion to the Virgin, the bishop commissioned a sculpted version of her image from Spain to be installed at the cathedral. The original image of the Virgin was created in an oil painting in which she looks down at the sleeping baby Jesus who lies in her lap. She is praying, and her hands are cupped over one of his. The original wooden carving replicating this image remained at the cathedral until 1920 when another, more magnificent carving was installed there.

In order to solidify the bond between the Virgin and the island's inhabitants, Pope Paul VI changed the date of her celebration to correspond with the date that held more significance on the island, November 19. This date was celebrated in Puerto Rico as the date the island was discovered. Coincidentally, there is evidence that one of the first Masses devoted to the Virgin of the Divine Providence was celebrated in Europe in 1744 on the same date. November 19 became the official feast day of the Virgin, who also became the island's official patroness. A 1996 newsletter published by the South East Pastoral Institute

(SEPI), *Documentaciones Sureste* discusses the significance and history of the patron Virgins of Latin America. It explains the decision by Pope Paul VI this way: "The intention was to join together the two great loves of the Puerto Ricans—love of their gorgeous island and love for the mother of God."

The pope's intentions were realized. Our Lady of the Divine Providence has become the principal religious icon on the island. Meléndez theorizes that it's the image of a loving, nurturing Virgin that captivated the population. "One can see the complete maternal and nurturing love of the Virgin Mary, where one sees the baby Jesus happily sleeping, with total trust and confidence, upon the lap of his mother. It is this same Divine Providence that resounds and echoes within the Puerto Rican soul a profound sense of harmony."

The Virgin Appears in New York

The growing Puerto Rican population in New York also felt the need to establish their devotion to Our Lady of the Divine Providence. Sonia Casanova, director of the Hispanic Ministry Office of the Catholic Diocese in New York, remembers how impressed she was as a little girl in Puerto Rico when she first beheld the image of the Virgin and took part in the celebration on November 19. She witnessed the deep devotion the Virgin inspired. "Hundreds of people would come to the shrine every day and say the rosary, and on Saturdays, they would say a whole *novena* (nine rosaries)." Many also believed that it was the Virgin who protected the island from hurricanes for twenty years after she was proclaimed patroness.

In Puerto Rico, it was common for the wooden likeness of the Virgin to tour the island before the statue was badly burned in 1980. It was sent to Spain to be repaired but has still not returned. In New York, artist Antonio Aviles was commissioned to create a statue of the Virgin. Like her counterpart on the island, this image would routinely tour the churches in the Archdiocese in

New York and the Diocese of Brooklyn. The pilgrimages took their toll on the statue, so it now has a permanent site at the Church of Saint Barbara in Brooklyn.

Although some churches organize their own celebrations each year, Casanova says the diocese hosts a central celebration, usually on a Friday. It features a Mass with a rosary and then a musical festival with food after the Mass. The diocese chose Friday over a Sunday event so that the liturgies would not conflict. The appeal of Our Lady of the Divine Providence is also growing, says Casanova. Each year, a more multicultural crowd attends the festivities.

FEAST DAY OF NUESTRA SEÑORA DE LA CARIDAD DEL COBRE

The Copper Virgin

AT THE beginning of the seventeenth century, Cuba had already been occupied by Spaniards for more than 100 years. In that time, the island had suffered catastrophic losses. Because of its position in the Caribbean, Cuba was strategically important for the Spaniards. Its rich land and mineral deposits, namely copper, held value, which forced the native inhabitants into slavery. When they died from disease and exhaustion, the Spaniards imported Africans to the island to supplement the slave work force.

The Catholic Church also sent its missionaries to convert the populace, but they would not be as effective on this island as they had been in other parts of Latin America. The time was ripe for the appearance of the Virgin of Charity.

According to testimony, two native Indian slaves—brothers Rodrigo and Juan de Hoyos—and a ten-year-old *negro esclavo* (black slave) called Moreno, had been employed by the copper mines at El Cobre, Cuba. They set out one day to find salt to be used at the mine to prepare food for the workers. Using an old boat, they rowed out across the Bay of Nipe to reach the salt deposits. Bad weather prevented them from completing the journey in one day, so they stopped at Cayo Francés. After a few days, the storm passed, the sun came out, and the sea was calm. As they approached their destination, they noticed something white floating on the sea. At first they thought it was a bird or a small girl, but they soon discovered that it was neither. What they found was a fifteen-inch statue of the Virgin Mary. Dressed in white, she was holding Jesus in her right arm and a gold cross in her left hand. The statue was attached to a piece of wood, which was inscribed with the words "Yo soy la Virgen de la Caridad (I am the Virgin of Charity.)" In his testimony years later, Moreno remarked that although it had been in the sea, neither the figure nor her clothing was wet.

There are many legends about "Cachita," as she's called. One states that she actually appeared to the three and saved them from the storm, but according to Father Mario Vizcaíno, Sch.P., of SEPI, author of *La Virgen de la Caridad: Patrona de Cuba* (Instituto Pastoral del Sureste: Miami), when Cuban scholar Leví Marrero began to research the legend of the Virgin in the 1970s, he discovered documents in Seville, Spain, that contained Moreno's written testimony about the experience. "In this document," says Vizcaíno, "we're able to confirm the data in the legend: there were three people in the boat, who they were, Moreno and the two Indian brothers, that they were not lost, and that they found the statue on a calm sea, not during the storm." The date of the discovery, April 1, 1612, was also confirmed by Moreno's testimony.

The statue was taken to the mining town of El Cobre, and eventually a shrine to her was built there. Her features, depicted on baked clay, have been called *mullatto* (dark), resembling the ethnic heritage of many Cubans. "It's also important who discovered her," says Vizcaíno. "The three slaves were all Cuban natives. This is very interesting because the blessed Mother chose to appear unto what was most Cuban at the time: Indians and a native slave, and they were of the lower classes. This is a pattern of the apparition of the Blessed Mother to appear to the most destitute in society and bring comfort."

The account was recorded in 1687, seventy-five years after the event took place. Moreno would have been eighty-five years old at the time. Although he confirms the sighting, Moreno's testimony does not explain how the statue got to the sea. Several scholars have postulated methods, many assuming that the Spaniards brought it with them. There already was a Virgin of Charity shrine in Illescas, Spain. Both virgins do resemble each other but have a few slight differences. Even if she was brought to the island by a colonist, she was quickly embraced by slaves because of the story and her appearance. In *Our Lady of the Exile: Diasporic Religion at a Cuban Catholic Shrine in Miami* (Oxford University Press, New York, 1997) author Thomas A. Tweed explains: "After the 1640s devotion to Our Lady of Charity spread. Slaves who worked in the copper mines around El Cobre seem to have venerated Our Lady of Charity during the earlier decades of the seventeenth century, at the hospital chapel, and in their homes; and then during the century's final decades, when the Virgin's image was pedestaled on the main altar of the Cobre shrine, devotion to Our Lady of Charity spread among the general population of the province of the Oriente."

Like the Virgin of Guadalupe in Mexico, Our Lady of Charity was used by Cubans as a source of inspiration and support during the thirty-year struggle for independence from Spain that began in 1868. Mothers prayed to her to protect their sons, and soldiers prayed to her to help them succeed. The clergy, however, remained divided over supporting the Crown or freedom for the island. Cubans would hold it against them and the church for years, but they did not hold it against the Virgin. Writes Tweed: "By the time the Spanish had been defeated (in 1898), the American occupying government had departed and an independent Cuban republic had been established (in 1902), the Virgin of Cobre had become 'la Virgen Mambisa.' She had become the rebel Virgin, the patriot Virgin, the national Virgin."

It was also a soldier's plea that would eventually convince Pope Benedict XV in 1916 to name her Cuba's national saint and establish her feast day.

Charita in Miami

Cuban migration to the United States is not a twentieth-century phenomenon. It began with the wars for independence in Cuba around 1868. Most of that population settled in outlying areas of Florida, such as Key West and Ybor City rather than Miami. That would soon change. What began as a trickle soon became a flood after the Communist takeover by Fidel Castro in 1959. According to the U.S. Census, the number of Cubans living in Dade County grew between 1960 and 1970 from 29,500 to 224,000.

Disenfranchised from their home country and learning to settle in a new country, with a new language and different culture, many Cubans looked to the Virgen de Caridad for support. Just as she was linked with Cuba's national identity in 1898, the Virgin became a necessary coping mechanism for Cuban exiles in the U.S. According to Tweed, ironically, the Virgin would help reinforce the Catholicism in many Cubans who traditionally had remained outside the Church. "Just as Cuban exiles in Key West and New York had appealed to Our Lady of Charity during the tumultuous 1890s, so too both of these contemporary migrants in Miami also emphasized the significance of devotion to the national patroness for making sense of the exile," writes Tweed.

The first organized Mass in Miami on the feast day of Our Lady of Charity was started in 1960 by Cuban priests. That first year, 800 devotees attended the mass. This was strong evidence of her appeal, but it was dwarfed the following year when a crowd of between 25,000 to 30,000 attended the mass for "Charita" held at Miami Stadium. The Catholic Church could not help but notice that kind of outpouring, but it wasn't until an Irish bishop from Pittsburgh, Archbishop Coleman F. Carroll, took over the parish that efforts to create a shrine to the Virgin escalated.

Many Cuban priests first resisted the effort, says Tweed. Many knew that the hold the church had on this congregation was tenuous and that the shrine would appeal to a devotion to the Virgin but negate the parish system, which reinforced Church doctrine. However, when Carroll announced his desire to build the shrine at a feast day Mass for the Virgin in 1965, the Cuban community responded eagerly. On December 2, 1973, in Miami, the shrine to Our Lady of Charity, La Ermita de la Caridad, was consecrated. Since then, the Virgin has been there for Miami's entire Latino community, including non-Catholics.

The Goddess Ochún

The story of the Spanish conquest is not a tranquil one. In many parts of Latin America, where the indigenous people outnumbered the Spanish, a cultural mixing, or *mestisaje,* occurred. Many Catholic rituals incorporated indigenous rites in an effort by the

The Rosary

The Virgin Mary loves and accepts everyone, even the poorest of the poor. The vast Marianite societies that exist to glorify her testify to the strength of her appeal. The Catholic Church invented a tool to focus prayer to the Virgin Mary, the rosary. Although it is erroneously thought of as just a piece of jewelry, the mechanism has a pattern of beads representing certain prayers: one "Glory Be to the Father," one "Apostles' Creed," five "Our Fathers" and fifty-three "Hail Marys." For a real experience of the feast of any Virgin, this is the tool that demonstrates true devotion.

There are three mysteries of the rosary—joyful, sorrowful, and glorious—that outline Mary's life as the mother of Jesus. Each mystery has five points that should be announced at the start of each decade of the rosary. Which mystery to focus on depends on the day of the week. Monday is assigned the joyful mysteries, Tuesday the sorrowful, Wednesday the glorious, and Thursday begins the cycle again.

The Mysteries
of the Rosary

Joyful

1. Annunciation
2. Visitation
3. Nativity
4. Presentation at the Temple
5. Finding in the Temple

Sorrowful

1. Agony of Jesus in the Garden
2. Scourging of Jesus at the Pillar
3. Crowning with Thorns
4. Carrying the Cross
5. Crucifixion

Glorious

1. Resurrection of Jesus
2. Ascension of Jesus
3. Descent of the Holy Spirit
4. Assumption of the Virgin Mary
5. Coronation of the Blessed Virgin Mary

priests to convert the population and an effort by the population to maintain their identity. This process has been called synchrotism. In Cuba, this *mestisaje* brought the Spanish, African, and indigenous cultures together. *Santería* became the dominant religion, obstructing efforts by the priests to establish a strong Church in Cuba. That struggle continues, even when it comes to the worship of the Virgin of Cobre.

The Virgin's alter ego in *santería* is Ochún, a Yoruba goddess. According to one legend, Ochún sympathized with the black slaves who were taken from their homes by the slave traders and forced to work in the mines and plantations in Cuba. She consulted her older sister, Yemayá, who told her that she could not stop the removal, so Ochún decided to follow her people to Cuba. But when her sister explained that not everyone in Cuba was black, Ochún asked her to grant two wishes—to make her skin lighter and her hair straighter so that all Cubans would like her. The statuette of the Virgin has an appearance like that of many Cuban women, with olive skin, dark hair, and dark eyes.

Regardless of her origin, the little statue in Miami, an exile herself, can still evoke impassioned responses. Many rafters who brave the ninety-mile stretch between Cuba and the U.S. depend on the Virgin to make the journey safely. But in Miami, "Our Lady of Charity evokes powerful responses," writes Tweed. "Devotees weep, smile, kneel, sing, wave, hope, complain, thank, and petition. She has the power to elicit such responses among Cuban exiles, I suggest, because they have consecrated her as a translocative and transtemporal symbol. . . . A second reason that the image in Miami evokes such a powerful response is that it positions devotees temporally. Our Lady of Charity stirs personal and collective memory."

On her journey to the United States, Maria del Carmen Cardenas prayed to the Virgin de Caridad del Cobre to protect her and her family. Like the original natives who first discovered the Virgin, Cardenas and her family had set out in a makeshift raft of old car seats and wood. They traveled through a storm and survived without water or food for three days. In a September 13, 1993, article in *The Record,* Cardenas, who settled in New Jersey with her family, believes that the Virgin heard her prayers. "It was our faith in her and in God that kept us alive. The Virgin protected us."

HOW TO SAY THE ROSARY

Step 1: Make the Sign of the Cross while saying: "In the name of the Father, of the Son, and of the Holy Ghost, Amen."

Step 2: While holding the crucifix at the beginning of the rosary, recite "The Apostles' Creed:"

I believe in God the Father Almighty, Creator of heaven and earth; and in Jesus Christ, His only Son, our Lord; Who was conceived by the Holy Ghost, born of the Virgin Mary, suffered under Pontius Pilate, was crucified, died, and was buried. He descended into hell; the third day He arose again from the dead; He ascended into heaven, and sitteth at the right hand of God, the Father Almighty; from thence He shall come to judge the living and the dead.

I believe in the Holy Ghost, the Holy Catholic Church, the communion of saints, the forgiveness of sins, the resurrection of the body, and life everlasting. Amen.

Step 3: On the next three beads, recite the "Hail Mary:"

Hail Mary, full of grace; the Lord is with thee: blessed art thou among women, and blessed is the fruit of thy womb, Jesus. Holy Mary, mother of God, pray for us sinners, now and at the hour of our death. Amen.

Step 4: At the next bead, say the "Our Father:"

Our Father, who art in heaven, hallowed be Thy name: Thy kingdom come: Thy will be done on earth as it is in heaven. Give us this day our daily bread: and forgive us our trespasses as we forgive those who trespass against us. And lead us not into temptation: but deliver us from evil. Amen.

Step 5: At the medallion that joins both ends of the rosary, say the "Glory Be to the Father:"

Glory be to the Father, and to the Son and to the Holy Ghost. As it was in the beginning, is now and ever shall be, world without end. Amen.

Step 6: Finish the rosary.

The rosary pattern begins at this point. Say the "Hail Mary" for each set of ten beads (decade) and an "Our Father" for the single bead between each set of ten. After the final "Hail Mary" in the fifth decade, recite this prayer, which ends the rosary:

"Oh God, whose only begotten Son, by his life, death, and resurrection has purchased for us the rewards of eternal life; grant, we beseech you, that while meditating on these mysteries of the most holy rosary, of the Blessed Virgin Mary, we may imitate what they contain and obtain what they promise through the same Christ our Lord. Amen."

This ends the rosary.

DÍA DE LA RAZA

The Flip Side of Columbus Day

ASK ANY schoolchild what October 12, 1492 means and you'll get the answer: the day that Christopher Columbus discovered America. But for many indigenous cultures in the United States and in Latin America, this date has a much different meaning. It represents a time when America was not "discovered" but when the lives of indigenous people, who already existed throughout the Americas and the Caribbean, were irreparably changed. For this reason, the celebration has taken on a more political tone.

Día de la Raza, or the Day of Our Race, is how Latin Americans refer to this date. When Latin Americans refer to "race," they're speaking of their Spanish and their indigenous roots, and October 12 becomes a day to celebrate that mixed heritage. Hispanics in the United States have embraced the day, however, as a time to primarily celebrate their indigenous roots, and as more historians reveal the true nature of that fateful trip from Spain to Santo Domingo in the Dominican Republic (where Columbus first landed), more and more people find the concepts behind Día de la Raza comforting.

Exceptional activities associated with Día de la Raza celebrations include indigenous dancing, spiritual cleansing, and mask making. The solemnity of the day is keenly felt, though, and for this reason, Día de la Raza has been used to promote causes and to educate people about the Hispanic heritage of this country.

Because Americans already celebrate Columbus Day, Día de la Raza has tremendous potential to cross over as a cultural celebration. In North America, the devastating impact on indigenous societies by European colonization was not only at the hands of the Spanish. The concept of Manifest Destiny gave the English a moral right to take over, usually by force, and vestiges of that attitude still survive. With this in mind, Columbus Day might become a day that includes consideration of the societies that existed in the New World and not just a day to recite a tale of three ships: the *Niña*, the *Pinta*, and the *Santa Maria*.

THE LATINO MARCH ON WASHINGTON

One of the most dramatic Día de la Raza celebrations took place in 1996. Two years earlier, California voters had passed Proposition 187, which denied social services like education and emergency medical care to illegal immigrants. This voter mandate signaled to Hispanics that intolerance towards them in this country had surfaced. When the federal government also enacted a welfare reform bill that denied services to legal immigrants, the line was drawn in the sand. Grassroots leaders felt that the government needed to know that Hispanics would not support any type of discrimination, so they planned a march on Washington.

On October 12, 1996, 100,000 Hispanics congregated on the nation's capital. They marched from the predominantly Hispanic Adams Morgan neighborhood down to the Ellipse behind the White House. Carrying signs that read, "We didn't land on Plymouth Rock, Plymouth Rock landed on us," and "Who is the immigrant, pilgrim?" the marchers hoped to emphasize their native ancestry, their ethnic pride, and solidarity. They used the concepts of Día de la Raza to dramatize their sense of empowerment. It was the largest group of Latinos to ever converge on the capital, and it demonstrated the power of Latino solidarity.

Who Owns Columbus?

To the mainstream United States culture, Columbus Day represents a day off of work and not much more. The most ceremony attached to the date happens in elementary schools, where teachers may pin up pictures of Columbus encountering members of the native Taino tribe that inhabited the Caribbean islands. In Italian American communities, however, Cristoforo Columbo, a native of Genoa, Italy, is very much honored. Parades and community festivals commemorate him, as do fraternal societies like the Knights of Columbus, a Catholic organization.

For U.S. Hispanics, there is some disagreement over Columbus's true legacy. Because of the desire to claim more evidence which traces the history of Hispanics in this country and confirms that it predates that of any other immigrant group, including the British and French, much is made of the Spanish ties to Columbus. Queen Isabella funded the enterprise, and although Columbus was born in Italy, he left as a young boy and adopted Spain as his home country. His writings were in Spanish, and legend has it that when he first saw land, he yelled, "*¡Tierra!*" which is Spanish for "land."

In New York City there is a friendly competition between the Hispanic and Italian American communities over which group has the better Columbus Day celebration. Established in 1944, the Italian American Columbus Day parade has a long history and has even become an important campaign stop for politicians who seek the Italian American vote. The Hispanic Columbus Day Parade has a shorter history—since 1964—but its organizers are just as fervent about their celebration. "We don't understand what the Italians celebrate," said parade organizer Elis Illescas in an October 14, 1996, *New York Times* article. "Everybody knows the discovery was a thoroughly Spanish event. Just look at us, what language do we speak? What do we look like? Italy had nothing to do with it."

In the same article parade chairman Frank G. Fusaro summed up the Italian American point of view. "I understand why the Hispanics want to associate themselves with Columbus," he says. "Some people also say he was Jewish. I think just about the only ones who have not claimed him are the Russians. But the fact of the matter is that he was Italian."

Día de la Raza looks at the underbelly of October 12, and this dichotomy was most keenly felt around the 500-year anniversary of the date of Columbus's landfall in 1992. The U.S. government assembled a committee, the Christopher Columbus Quincentenary Jubilee Commission, to plan a national celebration that would rival the country's bicentennial celebration sixteen years before. Spain, Columbus's host country, also got involved in the quincentennial by not only donating funds to the jubilee commission but also by sponsoring a world's fair devoted to Columbus's memory. Replicas of the three ships, *Niña, Pinta,* and *Santa Maria,* were built and docked in Seville and a second fleet of three replicas actually set sail and retraced the original voyage. The anniversary celebration in the United States, however, did not receive the same enthusiasm; in fact it was doomed.

Native American groups in both North and South America immediately protested. To glorify what happened in 1492 would ignore the great price paid by indigenous civilizations, they said. Countries in the Caribbean like Puerto Rico, Cuba, and the Bahamas have no native civilizations today. The Taino nation Columbus first encountered in the Caribbean was completely annihilated. The great Aztec civilization in Mexico, the Maya in Mexico and Central America, and the Incas in Peru withstood the Spanish invasion for a time, but eventually massive bloodshed brought about their final conquest. This kind of holocaust needed to be recognized, quincentennial opponents insisted.

Hans Koning wrote a biography of Columbus that was sharply critical of the explorer. In *Columbus: His Enterprise: Exploding the Myth* (Monthly Review Press: New York, 1991) he wrote, "It's almost obscene to celebrate Columbus because it's an unmitigated record of horror. We don't have to celebrate a man who was really—from an Indian point of view—worse than Attila the Hun." Even the National Council of the Churches of Christ urged the jubilee commission to keep a low profile on the celebration. "For the descendants of the survivors of the subsequent invasion, genocide, slavery, 'ecocide' and exploitation of the wealth of the land, a celebration is not an appropriate observance of this anniversary."

Some cities took aggressive action against the quincentennial. In California, Berkeley, Pasadena, Santa Cruz, and Oakland passed resolutions replacing Columbus Day with Indigenous People's Day. In North Dakota, Columbus Day was renamed Native American Day, and in 1992, Minneapolis, Minnesota, city officials passed a resolution that condemned Columbus and urged recognition instead of the legacy of Native Americans.

In Denver, Columbus Day celebrations had been sponsored by the city's Italian American community through the Knights of Columbus and the

Federation of Italian American Organizations of Colorado. However, as the five-hundredth anniversary approached, opposition to Columbus Day from the American Indian Movement (AIM) began to intensify and in recognition of their concerns, the Italian American community opted to cancel the traditional Columbus Day parade in Denver. The parade has not returned and probably never will, but Italian American groups in Denver have instigated a smaller event for the day as a fund-raiser for their organizations. "We're not disputing who got to America first. It's really a celebration for our Italian heritage," said Danny Rupoli in a 1997 *Denver Rocky Mountain News* article.

But for Hispanics, a celebration already existed that incorporated the cataclysmic cultural event from which they were born. In the spirit of Día de la Raza, a Latin American indigenous advocacy group, the Coordinating Body of the Indigenous People's Organizations of the Amazon Basin (COICA), organized peaceful, introspective events to commemorate the anniversary. They held what they called a "continental encounter" where they outlined ways to argue against quincentennial celebrations, which included creating an alternative Seville, in Mexico. "We want to recover our history, to affirm our identity, to achieve true independence from exploitation and aggression, and to play a role in determining our future," said Evaristo Nugkuag, president of COICA, in a 1991 *Time* article. The reaction to the quincentennial resulted in a name change for Día de la Raza to Día del Encuentro de Dos Mundos (Day of the Encounter of Two Worlds).

Some Latinos opted to focus on the present consequences of Columbus's trip rather than on its initial impact. Rather than single-mindedly lamenting the cultural loss at the hands of Columbus, some have searched for closure, for a way of reconciling what happened with the challenges facing Latinos today. Undeniably, some argued, Hispanics were born from this culture clash, so why not celebrate this uniqueness? For a few years after the quincentennial, emotions still raged every October 12. In a 1994 column for *National Minority Politics,* Roger E. Hernandez argued, "Columbus admirers term it the Discovery

Ojo de Dios

Día de la Raza is clearly unique among Latino holidays. Because of its serious tone, it is hard to link the day to any one activity, since it is more about introspection than overt celebration. The purpose of this day is to pay homage to the legacy of the native within every Latino in this country. In that spirit, there is an old indigenous handicraft, still taught to children—the *ojo de dios* (eye of God).

Created almost exclusively by the Huichol Indians in the Sierra Nevada Mountains near Jalisco, Mexico, the *ojo de dios* has great religious significance. It has the shape of a cross and is bound by yarn in the center, which is woven into the shape of a diamond. At the ends of the cross are smaller crosses, also bound by a diamond-shaped weave. "The *ojo de dios* is used to secure health and long life for the children. It is the wand—the eye—through which the eye of god will enter the supplicant," writes Marion Harvey in the book *Crafts of Mexico* (Macmillan Publishing Co., Inc.: New York, 1973).

of America; to his detractors it was the invasion; those who claim to be neutral sought a compromise and came up with the encounter." He continues: "Hispanics who condemn Columbus Day rightly condemn the butchery, but err when they claim they are simply victims of heartless European colonialism. They are, whether they like it or not, the cultural heirs of Spanish colonizers, not of colonized pre-Columbian civilizations."

Día de la Raza

In 1968, members of the Hispanic Caucus in Congress established Hispanic Heritage week. Exactly when U.S. Hispanics embraced Día de la Raza is unclear, but the holiday certainly gained visibility in 1988 when Congress expanded Hispanic Heritage week to a month-long celebration, September 15 through October 15, incorporating Día de la Raza. Associate professor of art history at the University of Texas at Austin Amelia Malagamba offers her theories regarding the evolution of Día de la Raza in this country: Much like the Columbus Day celebrations in the U.S., "Día de la Raza began as a date to commemorate 'the discovery' of America in Latin America as well," which carried more irony, says Malagamba, since it was in a sense "a celebration of the conquest, the annihilation of the populace but also a recognition of the *mestizaje* (clash of two cultures that produced a new race)."

The holiday became a general practice through school curricula, which taught children about the voyage of Columbus to the Americas. "Where it becomes more widespread is in the 1950s and 1960s with the publication of the *Libro de Texto Unico* which was provided by the [Mexican] government, which celebrated the coming of Columbus to the Americas," Malagamba explains. "This text provided a standardized description of what children would learn about Columbus."

Another book of a completely different nature also caught on among many philosophers and activists at the time: *La Raza Cósmica,* by José Vasconcelos. This treatise espoused the commonality shared by Latin America, which the author described as a single huge continent united by a common language and history because of Columbus. This planted the seed of cultural pride and added a political connotation to the word *raza*, which literally means "race" but was expanded to include ethnicity and skin color. At this point the concepts of Columbus and *raza* became separate and distinct.

In the United States, between the 1930s and 1940s, another social experience was developing that would also affect perceptions in Mexico and parts of Latin America—the *pachuco* movement. "*Pachuco*" was a Spanish word used to describe lower-class Mexican Americans who sported a cool attitude and a unique sense of style. Their children would become zoot suiters decades later. The word evolved to define a movement, says Malagamba, when many of these men

Although the Huichol were somewhat influenced by Christianity, the shape of the cross is not a Christian reference, adds Harvey, but rather, it represents the four directions or the four elements: earth, fire, water, and air.

To begin to make an *ojo de dios,* choose bright, beautiful colors but no more than three. The yarn should be one-ply, and you will need about two skeins, or one for each color. Before trying to make the more complex cross with five stars, practice by making one cross with the diamond pattern in the center. You will need two dowels, one that is 15 inches long and one that is 25 inches long. They should be one-fourth inch in diameter.

Steps:

1. Line up 25-inch and 15-inch dowels so that they are parallel and flush at one end. Without knotting it, wrap the yarn (about six times) around the dowels at the middle of the shorter dowel. Then twist the dowels at right angles so that they make a cross.

2. Check to see if the center of the diamond is as large as you want it.. The

yarn should be tight but not so much that the dowels pull in one direction or another.

3. To make a large center of the diamond, start from the beginning and simply wrap the yarn around the two dowels several more times before twisting them into a cross.

4. After building the desired center and twisting the dowels, begin weaving by winding the yarn under and over the center dowel, moving counterclockwise the next dowel. Keep the yarn taut and make sure the strands line up together and don't overlap.

5. To switch colors, cut or break off the yarn but don't tie it off to the dowel. Connect that end to the end of the next color with a square knot and twist the slack of the first color around a dowel before beginning to weave again, to conceal the knot.

6. Continue weaving until the center diamond is between 2 1/2 to 3 inches wide or until you've achieved the desired size of *ojo*. Finish off the cross by winding the yarn down the center dowel a few times before knotting it.

began serving in the armed forces in World War II and returned home to be treated as less than citizens. In Texas, the American GI Forum, an organization that still fights for the rights of Hispanic veterans, was born at this time. When a local funeral home refused to handle the body of decorated veteran Felix Longoria, Dr. Hector Garcia enlisted the help of U.S. Senator Lyndon Baines Johnson, who got Longoria buried with honors at Arlington National Cemetery. Garcia went on to found the American GI Forum. "The *pachucos* were struggling for recognition," says Malagamba. "Their identities became synonymous with the word *raza,* and their language (words like *carnal, ese,* and *vato*) became the language of the poor."

In Mexico, comedians began copying the lingo as well and coining the question, "*¿Eres tu raza?* (Are you *raza*?)," which changed the word *raza* to signify the masses. The question really has several layers, says Malagamba. "It asks, 'Hey you. Are you part of who I am? If so, then you can come with me.'" This attitude paved the way for Día de la Raza, in Latin America and for Latino communities in the United States, to change from a Columbus Day celebration into something completely different.

In the 1960s and 1970s, the Chicano Movement began to question the status quo, and although it was a political movement, it was also a social one. The main mission of the Chicano Movement was Latino empowerment. To achieve this, Latinos had to be encouraged to reach back to their indigenous roots, to the people who inhabited and civilized the Americas, not to the people who came from Europe and conquered them. Because the movement was anti-Eurocentric, Día de la Raza offered a means of promoting the Chicano philosophy by focusing on the indigenous heritage of Latinos. "It became a celebration of us, of who we are today," says Malagamba.

According to Ramon Vasquez y Sanchez of the Centro Cultural de Aztlan in San Antonio, the reason Latinos celebrate Día de la Raza is to recognize "that you are the people of the western hemisphere. Día de la Raza celebrates our roots, that our roots are here [in the Western Hemisphere]. Until recently, anything to do with the Indian was always given a negative connotation. The Chicano Movement wanted to change that by looking at the civilization that existed before the Spanish arrived."

The celebration held (and still holds) particular appeal to grassroots organizations like the United Farm Workers (UFW) union, which used the day to rally supporters. The UFW proposed that farm workers embodied the indigenous relationship with the earth and its legacy of food products like corn, tomatoes, potatoes, chocolate, and coffee. Día de la Raza is still used politically to bring attention to the fact that for many dark-skinned Latinos, the effects of the conquest—discrimination and neglect—still persist.

7. Once you feel confident with the weaving process, you can add the smaller diamonds, using four shorter dowels that are each 3 3/4 inches long.

8. Repeat steps two through five for the smaller diamonds, positioning them at the outside edge of the previously woven center part.

9. When finishing the smaller diamonds, wind the yarn down the dowel toward the center diamond and knot it in the back.

10. When the *ojo* is complete, the dowels should be concealed by yarn and the knots concealed at the back.

Once you've mastered the weaving technique, there are variations to try, such as adding texture by flipping the cross and weaving on the backside. This technique is great for monochromatic patterns. Also, tassels at the ends finish off the *ojo de dios* nicely.

Día de la Raza Today

Most Día de la Raza celebrations focus on indigenous values, like an appreciation of the Earth, and learning the names of the Aztec leaders as well as the Spanish conquistadors who followed after Columbus. Traditional indigenous dances and ceremonies are also reenacted as part of the celebration. "The mood is still somber on Día de la Raza," says Malagamba. "It recognizes the dying of natives but also the dialectic resolution of accepting the *mestizaje*. Those who identify with being part of *la raza* are part of that experience."

Most Día de la Raza celebrations highlight themes of empowerment, spirituality, and history. This is a day Hispanics choose to reaffirm their cultural pride for the part of them that has been overlooked or forgotten.

DÍA DE LOS MUERTOS

Celebrating Death, Celebrating Life

AN INDIGENOUS Mexican celebration, Día de los Muertos (The Day of the Dead), November 2, should not be confused with Halloween, October 31, All Saint's Day, November 1, or All Soul's Day, November 2. Instilled into the native populations of Mexico by Spanish missionaries, the holiday does share a date and the same religious overtones as All Soul's Day, but its roots are firmly planted in native folklore and tradition. As the native populations attempted to assimilate the teachings of the Catholic priests with their own religious rites, a clash of spiritual energies was inevitable. Thus, the Day of the Dead was started by the Mexican native tribes as a means of continuing their belief in the circle of life in which death plays a part and is not to be feared. As it evolved, the native holiday incorporated aspects of the Catholic teaching of death as an end to mortal life and a beginning of a new and better afterlife.

In Mexico, this holiday is celebrated at night and in cemeteries. The family of the departed makes offerings of food and drink and places the traditional flowers, marigolds, at each gravesite. During this offering, the family members also offer prayers or speak to the dead. In the United States, many Mexican American families make a pilgrimage to family gravesites with offerings of flowers, but during the day, not at midnight. *Ofrendas,* or altars, are built inside many homes. They contain significant objects that the departed relative might have cherished as reminders of the deceased. Candles are lit and prayers are offered at the *ofrendas* as well.

CALAVERAS EVERYWHERE

The most important character on Día de los Muertos (Day of the Dead) is the key symbol of *death*, the *calavera*. This word means skull or skeleton. These skeleton images are not ghastly, but symbolic of life. In fact, they help the living embrace the circle of life. Mexican curios that feature skeletons employed in some kind of diversion done normally by the living—like playing in a band or washing dishes—express a whimsical rather than sinister view of death. The *calavera* shows up everywhere, even in the traditional food of the day, *pan de muerto,* a sweet bread molded into the shape of a skull and baked with a plastic skeleton inside. Similarly, the traditional sugar skull confections bear the same image, as does *papel picado* (paper streamers made up of rectangular sections that have been cut out, similar to paper snowflakes, to depict the skeleton in different scenes).

The Day of the Dead is one of the more mystical Hispanic celebrations, and it can be the most fulfilling. It represents a clash of pagan and Christian beliefs, but its message of death as a continuance, not an end, can be uplifting. The true, irresistible nature of this tradition is appealing to more and more non-Latinos, especially in the Southwest.

The Laughing Skeleton

Cultural differences can impede participation in a cultural celebration, especially one that is unfamiliar. When traveling in a foreign country, tourists usually perceive cultural differences immediately. For example, in India, the cow is revered, even pampered, and most importantly, never eaten. To own a cow is a status symbol, and families will sacrifice to maintain the animal. In the

United States, however, the same animal is seen as unintelligent and worthy of nothing more than being eaten. The species has even been bred to increase its size so that it can produce more meat.

Within the United States, some cultural traditions are respected even when they differ from American habits. When eating at a Japanese restaurant, for example, it is the custom to remove your shoes. American patrons don't question it and will observe the custom. Yet, being shoeless in a restaurant is clearly an American faux pas, reinforced daily by most mainstream American restaurants, which proudly hang a sign that reads, "No shoes, no shirt, no service."

For newcomers to the celebration of the Day of the Dead, the biggest cultural stumbling block will be the day's key symbol, the *calavera*. But an understanding of the importance of the *calavera* enhances the experience of the Day of the Dead because skeleton icons take on a considerable significance on this day, not as the markers of death but as a symbol of the circle of life. Clay art, sugar skull confections, *pan de muerto,* and *papel picado* all bear the image of the skeleton.

In this country, the skeleton carries an eerie reputation, usually associated with Halloween images of ghosts, goblins, and ghouls. It represents death universally, whether depicted as the Grim Reaper, uncovered at an archaeological site, or examined at a crime scene. Skeletons are literally the last remnants of our physical bodies and our last link to life on Earth. In fact, they're a discomforting reminder of how fragile the human body is and how fleeting is life. Perhaps this is why the skeleton elicits a negative reaction in most Americans.

To understand the Day of the Dead, the skeleton image must be approached with a sense of humor. It might help to translate the word to Spanish and call it the *calavera.* In Mexico, especially in the state of Oaxaca, which is famous for its extravagant Day of the Dead celebration, the *calavera* is still very much attached to the soul of the person who walked in it while alive and whose memory lives in the minds of relatives and friends.

Most importantly, the *calavera* is used as a tool. Although the Aztecs approached dying differently, as part of life and not the end to life, they still respected death and possibly gained some fear of it once the Spaniards began to instill their Christian beliefs. Mexicans use the *calavera* to help them face the fear by dressing it in traditional costumes and depicting it in paintings, dancing, laughing, or engaging in any of the activities the individual would have performed in life. Rarely is the *calavera* depicted in a menacing manner; instead it is seen in humdrum and even humorous settings.

The most common curios sold in Mexico depicting these scenes (they can be purchased in some parts of the United States, especially in the Southwest), are called *calacas*. Fans of the television show *Northern Exposure* may remember that the character Maggie O'Connell used *calacas* in an *ofrenda* to her dead boyfriends. *Calacas* come in all sizes and can be made of plaster, clay, or papier-mâché, and can depict the *calavera* in a variety of life-like activities—dressed as a musician, a beautician, or a dentist, for example.

Miniatures made of clay and wire and called *escenas* are also quite popular. Similarly, they usually depict a scene or activity in life. In an *escena,* a miniature diorama, musicians play instruments, bakers bake, secretaries type, and husbands cheat on their wives. Compound this folk art activity with the *pan de muerto,* the sugar *calavera* candy, *papel picado,* paintings, earrings, and puppets made in the *calavera* image, and clearly, skeletons are inescapable on the Day of the Dead and must be accepted as part of the celebration.

Printmaker José Guadalupe Posada, whose prints eventually inspired the work of Mexican muralists Manuel Orozco and Diego Rivera, produced a popular representation of the *calavera*. Born February 2, 1852, in Aguascalientes, Mexico, Posada was surrounded by artisans. His father was a baker and his uncle was a potter. Posada's own work as a lithographer was considered groundbreaking, especially considering that his development in the field came when printmaking had been all but abandoned in Mexico. The images he chose and the boldness of his political satire also distinguished him. At times, the *calaveras* in his prints take on a sinister attitude, representing the oppressed society in which Mexicans existed during the dictatorial presidency of Porfirio Díaz. Generally, Posada remained true to the nature of the holiday, and his *calaveras* usually depicted people doing everyday things, from making love to drinking a beer. He portrayed the common and the famous man alike as *calaveras*, from street cleaners to revolutionaries like Emiliano Zapata.

In a 1995 article in *Hispanic* magazine, René Arceo, special projects director at the Mexican Museum in Chicago, explained the phenomenon to writer Yleana Martinez. "To the Mexican, life is death and death is life. [It is] one unit, one part. That differs from the way it is seen by most Western civilizations, where life and death never meet. It is not the way it is seen in Mexico, where the indigenous people understood Nature and that they were part of it. They learned from the cycles of life." Mexicans owe this lesson to the Aztecs.

All Souls' Day Reinvented

Although the Day of the Dead was established in Mexico by the Aztecs, Spanish missionaries saw it as similar to All Souls' Day, the day set aside by the Catholic Church to remember the dead. The Aztecs had already incorporated the dead into their theology, so they easily accepted the concept of setting aside a day to remember those who had passed. Some scholars credit the missionaries for their ability to merge Catholic celebrations with those of the native tribes. But that's about as far as the missionaries got. Some celebrations never lost their indigenous soul, and the Day of the Dead is one of them.

The Aztecs were the dominant society in Mexico when the Spaniards arrived in the fifteenth century. They began as a nomadic tribe but established themselves in the valley of Mexico (Mexico City) at the end of the twelfth century and established the capital city of Tenochtitlán. They were supposedly led to this spot by their rain god, Huitzilopochtli, who told them to settle in the spot were they found a snake being devoured by an eagle. This was the Anahuac Valley, and its swampy terrain helped make the Aztecs impervious to invaders while they built their empire. This legend of the eagle and snake survived and is featured on Mexico's flag.

The Aztecs had their own history of conquests, including the Toltecs, Mixteca-Puebla, and Zapotec. In order to stave off any bad karma, they incorporated traditions of offering sacrifices to the gods, including humans. By the time the Spaniards arrived, the Aztecs had reconciled their view of death as a circle of life and had incorporated their own festivals to honor that belief. The Aztecs believed that the dead still endured trials and challenges in the afterlife as part of their journey to peace. But even so, death was viewed as a release from even greater trials and challenges encountered in life. Traditionally at funerals, the living made offerings and encouraged the dead on their way to the final resting place. Since they believed that spirits could return to earth and influence the living, the Aztecs celebrated a feast day when the dead and living reunited.

It was not a great leap for the missionaries to combine the two celebrations, but although they seemed to gain a toehold for Christianity at the time, the celebration retained the Aztec philosophy. The missionaries wrote of rituals directed at the god of death, Mictlantecuhtli, and of how the ritual persevered even after the conquest. The practice of building an *ofrenda,* which is considered a threshold between heaven and earth, brings the reunion between the living and dead into the home. Making things to eat and toys to play with on November 2 takes the fear out of dying, especially for children, and gives the day a cheerful atmosphere. It also welcomes the dead back by providing recognizable objects and offering their favorite food. Designating a flower like the marigold as part of the tradition balances the party atmosphere with symbolism and respect.

Build your Own *Ofrenda*

To build an altar in the home, decide first if you want the altar to honor one person or a group of family members. Once you choose, the altar will need a focal point, usually a photograph, but it can also be an object that represents your loved one, like a trophy, a tool from his or her profession, or some kind of artwork. The central piece is the most important because the *ofrenda* will be built around it.

Next choose a location. You may prefer to build it outside, but find a location that won't be disturbed by children or pets. It could be on a mantel, a bookshelf, or a plant stand. Start building in October. You can begin with just a photo, but try to add to it every day other objects that remind you of that person. Add a book, a CD, jewelry, a guitar pick, an amulet—anything that relates to that person's personality—until you arrange a nice collection of things around your centerpiece. Family members can even include personal notes to the loved one. Leave room for the candles, which should not be lit until November 1 and which should stay lit until

The Art of Day of the Dead

Planning a family trip to the cemetery may not be for everyone, but there is an option that can ease a newcomer into the Day of the Dead celebration. Folk art and fine art rule this day, so many art organizations have incorporated the date into their exhibit calendars. Some organizations focus on printed artwork, which may include the work of Posada. Others focus on what may be the earliest form of installation art, the *ofrenda*.

Galería de la Raza in the Mission District of San Francisco has organized a community celebration of Day of the Dead since 1972. There are two components of the celebration: an *ofrenda* exhibit and a procession from the gallery to Garfield Park. "The celebration has evolved into a very multicultural one," says Jaime Cortez, program manager for the gallery. "Don't expect to see a traditional Día de los Muertos event. You'll see people from all different cultures sharing a part of their cultural tradition regarding the dead."

Artist Rene Yañez began the exhibit by building the first *ofrenda* at the center. He initially modeled it after the traditional customs in Oaxaca, with marigolds, food offerings, and *papel picado*. From that exhibit grew bigger and bigger *ofrendas* created by artists, community members, and schoolchildren. These have become less traditional but more communal. The procession is an extension of the *ofrenda* exhibit and was organized as a response to a perceived need to recognize lost loved ones. It was also encouraged by the fact that by city ordinance, there is no cemetery located in the heart of San Francisco. The nearest one is found outside of the city, in Colma, California, nearly thirty miles away. This distance made it prohibitive for the community to visit a cemetery, so the procession helped fill that requirement. "This began because there was a need in our community to honor the tradition and to honor the dead," says Yañez.

Across the bay in Oakland there was a similar need, but as the Galería event grew, the Oakland Hispanic community felt a need to return to a more spiritual celebration. When the Oakland Museum of Art set up its Latino Advisory Board in 1994, one of its first suggestions was to sponsor a Day of the Dead event. "The board members felt there was a real need in the community to not only host such an event on their side of the Bay but also to try to maintain the tradition for future generations of Latinos," says Barbara Henry, chief curator at the Oakland Museum of Art. "Many members of the board felt the tradition had been lost."

To capture the spirit of the event, planners focused on a strong educational as well as a cultural component and recruited a guest curator, Beatrice Carrillo Hocker. Like the Galería observance, the Day of the Dead exhibit at the museum initially focused on the *ofrenda*. Again, it was not just artists who created the installations; members of the community and schoolchildren were also invited to create *ofrendas*. Since then, the museum has expanded the event beyond an art exhibit to a multidisciplinary spiritual event. Performances were added in the form of *ceremonias*. Local spiritual leaders present *ceremonias* that are drawn from the original Aztec ceremony—from burning sage in a purification ritual to traditional dances—and that helped reinforce the day's indigenous roots.

midnight November 2. Choose safe candles and avoid placing them too close to flammable objects in the *ofrenda*.

Marigolds are the traditional flower to add to the *ofrenda*, but you can choose a flower that is more closely associated with the deceased. Flowers and food items can be added at the last minute. Choose a time of day to gather the family on November 2 to think about and honor your loved one. Keep the *ofrenda* up after El Día de los Muertos is over. Each year, add new components, maybe even some *calacas* or *escenas*.

"Education is an important part of our event," says Carillo Hocker. "We're very careful that our event maintains the traditional qualities of the celebration."

The museum also provides hands-on activities so you can carry the celebration home. Each year, a community memorial marigold flower arch is built in the style of those created in Oaxaca. Members of the community are invited to write a dedication card to a loved one, attach it to a marigold, and place it on the arch. Workshops are held to instruct participants on how to make ceremonial objects such as rattles, which were made from dried gourds and clay, skull masks, *calavera* puppets, and Mexican-style tin photo frames to place in an *ofrenda*. For those interested in learning how to make traditional food for an *ofrenda,* the event even includes a tortilla-making demonstration.

The Día de los Muertos is now a regular event and the most popular one at the museum, attracting 2,500 people. "The need to share grief is still a very strong urge which attracts more people to this celebration," Henry concludes. "Día de los Muertos appeals to the human experience—the sense of loss and grief—while celebrating life as well."

In the literature about the Galería de la Raza's Día de los Muertos celebration, professor Amalia Mesa-Bains wrote, "Memory which celebrates death ultimately strengthens life. Remembrance and ceremony form a reality that has strengthened a community. The celebration of Día de los Muertos has been an ongoing recognition of a life force tied to its own death and history. Like an unending cycle of cultural continuity," she concluded, "the Chicano Day of the Dead is a gesture of the ephemeral, forever changing, forever beginning."

Death can be hard to take. Too many times, grieving over the end of life reinforces its finality and leaves mourners without comfort. Día de los Muertos offers that comfort. Real or not, it gives the bereaved an opportunity to become immersed in thoughts of a lost loved one and even to imagine that that loved one has paid them a visit. Ironically, even though many church doctrines, including Christianity, espouse a life after death, Día de los Muertos makes it seem more real.

WINTER

Advent and a Fresh Start

~

DECEMBER 12
THE FEAST OF THE VIRGIN OF GUADALUPE

~

DECEMBER 24 AND 25
NOCHE BUENA AND LA NAVIDAD

(Christmas Eve and Christmas Day)

~

JANUARY 6
DÍA DE LOS REYES

INVIERNO

THE HOLIDAY SEASON swirls around Christmas and New Year's Day, and for many Latinos this is a time of religious fervor, neighborhood connections, and family unity. Winter brings in the religious time of year associated with Christ's birth, called Advent, which contains the important holidays of Christmas and the Epiphany. Advent, like Lent, is a long period of time beginning four Sundays before Christmas and observed by some Christians as a season of prayer and fasting.

Before Christmas, in early December, preparations begin to honor the Virgin of Guadalupe. This *virgen*'s feast day is December 12. She is a

Mexican icon, the "Mother of the Americas," and a symbol of the marriage of indigenous and European belief.

Celebration of nochebuena (Christmas Eve) is an enduring tradition in the Hispanic community, while Christmas remains a joyful and holy time. La Navidad (Christmas) is the climax of the holiday season and the year, but the Epiphany, or Día de Los Reyes, also carries great importance. Why do many houses in Hispanic neighborhoods keep their Christmas decorations up after New Year's Day? The answer is simple. It's because for them Christmas isn't over on December 25; instead, the season ends twelve days later, on January 6.

Known in English as the Epiphany, Three Kings' Day, Feast of the Magi, and in Spanish as Los Reyes Magos and Día de los Reyes, the date signifies and celebrates the arrival of the three kings into Bethlehem to view the Christ child. This holiday has nearly vanished in mainstream celebrations, but remains significant to many Latinos. Focused on children, it ends the Christmas season on a note of promise as the New Year begins.

DECEMBER 12

FEAST OF THE VIRGIN OF GUADALUPE

Revered Mother for a Native People

THE STORY of Our Lady of Guadalupe is remembered each year on her feast day, which is celebrated on December 12. She embodies the clash between the indigenous people of Mexico and the Catholic Church. Initial resistance to the work of many Catholic missionaries and their muscle, the conquistadors, proved dangerous to native Mexicans, usually ending in their bloodshed and loss of life. In an effort to salvage some vestige of their culture, the natives embraced a dark-skinned Virgin who chose to appear to an Indian man rather than to one of the Catholic monks. Even her message was delivered in the Indians' native Náhuatl tongue and not Spanish.

This holiday is a time of reflection and appreciation for true believers. Like other feast days commemorating saints and Virgins, local churches handle the preparation and planning for the procession, Mass, and feast, a chance for each congregation to feel more connected to their faith. As a church-related holiday, the "celebration" of the Virgin of Guadalupe varies with communities but the celebration of her image occurs all year long.

MORE THAN JUST A PRETTY FACE

In recent years, the Virgin of Guadalupe has become a trendy symbol to mainstream consumers and non-Catholics. Many boutiques and shops that sell decorative home accessories carry something—a jewelry box, refrigerator magnet, or votive candle—bearing the image of the Virgin of Guadalupe. Nuestra Señora de Guadalupe (Our Lady of Guadalupe), or, as she's known to Latinos, *la Virgen de Guadalupe*, stands serenely in a radiant golden oval aura, wearing a rose-colored gown over which is draped a star-spangled blue satin cloak. Often depicted surrounded by her signature roses, she is a strong, feminine symbol who touches many. But what is more important, and what main-

stream consumers may not realize, is that this venerable icon

represents a cultural affirmation of Mexico and its indigenous

people. Mother of the Americas, she is the only Virgin whose

apparition has appeared in the Western Hemisphere.

The Story of Juan Diego

According to Guadalupe scholars, evidence of native worship of a *virgen* figure predates the official account of her apparition by more than a century. The Virgin's visit was officially documented and published in 1649 by the vicar of her shrine, Luis Laso de la Vega. An account in Spanish by another priest, Miguel Sánchez, was published before de la Vega's, but the latter is considered official because it is an interpretation of an account written by the natives in their own language, Náhuatl. Many scholars still argue over the authenticity of the story. In her book *Our Lady of Guadalupe: Faith and Empowerment among Mexican-American Women* (University of Texas Press: Austin, Texas, 1994), Jeanette Rodriguez cites the opinion of the late Náhuatl scholar Angel Garibay, who concluded that de la Vega's account stems from several sources, some of whom are closely associated to the actual event, beginning with the interpreter used by Juan Diego and Bishop Juan Gonzalez de Zumárriga.

The story begins outside Mexico City on the morning of December 9, 1531, when a recently converted middle-aged Aztec Indian named Juan Diego is walking to an early mass. He hears birds singing so beautifully that he believes he is hallucinating and in paradise. He hears a woman's voice calling his name, and when he follows the voice, it leads him to the top of a hill called Tepeyac, where he encounters an apparition. It is the image of a woman who seems to glow. Her dress is radiant and her expression reveals love and compassion. She tells Juan Diego that she is the Virgin Mary and that she needs a temple built on that site and that he must send this message to the bishop so that he will get it built.

She said: "I have a living desire that there be built a temple, so that in it I can show and give forth all my love, compassion, help, and defense, because I am your loving mother: to you, all who are with you, to all the inhabitants of this land and to all who are with you, to all the inhabitants of this land and to all who love me, call upon me, and trust in me. I will hear their lamentations and will remedy all their miseries, pains, and sufferings."

Juan Diego complies with her wishes, but when he reaches the palace of the Spanish bishop, Juan de Zumárriga, he is made to wait. When he does get to see the bishop, Zumárriga does not believe him. Juan Diego returns to the site where the Virgin visited him and finds her waiting for him. He tells her that the bishop ignored him and pleads with her to choose a more notable person to be her messenger, someone who is respected and will be believed. The Virgin is not swayed and asks Juan to visit the bishop again the next day and repeat her message.

On his second attempt, Juan again has to wait to see the bishop, but this time Zumárriga asks him for more details. He asks Juan Diego to describe the Virgin, where she appeared, what she wore, and what she said. Although Juan Diego answers completely, the bishop decides that his word is not good enough and asks him to bring proof that he has met with the Virgin. Juan returns to Tepeyac to report his second attempt to the Virgin, who responds:

"Very well, my son, you will return here tomorrow so that you may take to the bishop the sign that he has asked for. With that, he will believe you and will have no further doubts; and know well, my beloved son, that I will repay you for your care, work, and fatigue which you have done on my account."

The next day, Juan Diego is called to visit his uncle who was dying. He spends a day looking for a doctor to tend to his uncle, but failing to find one, accepts that his uncle is near death. Diego races back to Tlatelolco to find a priest to administer the last rites. On the morning of December 12, 1531, Juan Diego sets out to find a priest. He tries to avoid the hill, feeling that his uncle needs immediate attention, but the Virgin finds him. Embarrassed, Juan Diego tells her that he did not wish to displease her but that his uncle needed him. With compassion for his concerns, the Virgin assures him that his uncle will not die, and that he has in fact been cured.

With Juan Diego free of worry about his uncle, the Virgin instructs him to gather flowers growing on top of a nearby hill and take them to the bishop. When Diego locates the site with flowers referred to by the Virgin, he is amazed to find it covered with roses, an unusual flower to be growing wild in a desert. He gathers the flowers, takes them to the Virgin, who then places them in his cloak, or *tilma*. She instructs him not to open his cloak until he is in the presence of the bishop.

When he arrives at the bishop's palace, the bishop's servants again make him wait. They even try to take the roses, but Juan Diego is resolute. When he finally gets to see the bishop, he relates his latest visit with the Virgin and at this point, he lets the roses drop from his cloak, only to find that imprinted on it is a picture of the Virgin. This miracle is proof enough for the bishop to finally believe the peasant. Juan Diego's *tilma* remains on view to this day in the shrine built for the Virgin of Guadalupe at Tepeyac.

The Holy Image

Next to the story itself, the most powerful thing about this "brown" Virgin's appearance is the physical proof that reveals her image. Like the Shroud of Turin, the *tilma* has been subjected to rigorous physical tests, which confirm its authenticity. The power of the *tilma* as a self-portrait of the Virgin is evident from the droves of the faithful who visit her shrine outside Mexico City every day, but particularly on December 12. Writes Jacqueline Orsini Dunnington in her book *Guadalupe, Our Lady of New Mexico*: "The miraculous portrait is preserved in a hermetically sealed frame in the new basilica, and is viewed annually by millions of people who look at it from a moving walkway. No early document related to her commands this degree of respect; no hymn or ballad carries her symbolism with an equal impact; no oration or folktale has the force of this visual image, its copies and applications."

The image of this Virgin is quite unique. Unlike the more ornate and regal images of the Virgin Mary found in parts of Europe, Guadalupe reveals an understated regality. Her head is tilted to the left and her greenish eyes are cast downward. Her skin is olive and her hair black. Her mantle, which covers her head and shoulders, is a striking deep turquoise, and she wears a rose-colored gown. According to chemical tests on the *tilma,* these components of the image are original.

As early as 1666, a group of artists who studied the image concluded that it could not have been created by human hands. They felt the representation was too finely painted on the coarse canvas of the *tilma* to have been done by any known artist. They proclaimed the *tilma* divine. As recently as 1981, two scientists, Phillip Serna Callahan and Jody Brant Smith, tested the cloak using infrared technology. In his report printed in the Center for Applied Research in the Apostate (CARA) Studies on Popular Devotion, Callahan says, "There is no way either to explain the kind of color pigments utilized or the maintenance of color and brightness of the pigments over the centuries.

Furthermore, when consideration is given to the fact that there is no under-drawing, sizing, or over-varnish, and that the weave of the fabric is itself utilized to give the portrait depth, no explanation of the portrait is possible by infrared techniques." Other parts of the image, however, like the angel at the Virgin's feet, the black crescent moon, the stars on her mantle, the mantle's gold trim, and her glowing aura, have been added.

Perhaps the most bizarre results have emerged from tests on her eyes. Between 1950 and 1980, several ophthalmologists used infrared photography to photograph her eyes and then analyze the image on a computer. They actually discovered a human bust revealed in her eyes. Both eyes contain images, and while the identities of these people have not been proven, the experts hypothesize that one image is that of Juan Diego, the second is of the bishop and the third of a black woman who may have been a slave held by the bishop. Whoever the people are, they represent a blending of races.

Virgin Worship Worldwide

A long history is attached to the uniquely Catholic tradition of Virgin worship. The Mexican Virgen de Guadalupe is not the first miraculous witnessing of a Virgin, nor is she even the first Virgen de Guadalupe. The first celebration of this Virgin began in Spain, and even the root of the name "Guadalupe" is Arabic, the language of the Moors (although there have been attempts to link it to Náhuatl, the language of the Aztecs).

The adoration of the Virgin continues to evolve. The first recorded tribute to Mary happened in A.D. 431 at the third Ecumenical Council in Turkey, where Mary was declared the mother of God. More recently, six children in Bosnia and Herzegovina claimed to have seen visions of the Virgin beginning in 1981 and continuing through 1997. Other famous Virgins include the Virgin of the Immaculate Conception, who appeared eighteen times at a grotto near

Lourdes, France in 1858, and Our Lady of Fatima, who appeared to three children in Fatima, Portugal, six times between the spring and fall of 1917. Wherever the Virgin has been reported with some credibility to have appeared, her shrine attracts many visitors.

Veneration of a female deity was not a totally new concept to the Aztecs, who already worshipped a similar though less benign goddess named Tonantzin. But what makes Our Lady of Guadalupe more extraordinary and tangible than all other patroness Virgins is the physical evidence of the shroud that she left behind.

While U.S. celebrations are localized, in Mexico the holiday is huge, centered on the Virgin's shrine in Mexico City. Thousands make the pilgrimage to Mexico City to view the *tilma* bearing her image. She is known by a number of other names, including La Madrecita (little mother), la Virgen de Tepeyac, La Virgencita (little *virgen*), and Queen of the Americas. As Dunnington explains, the *virgen*'s multiple names reveal the intensity of her appeal. "Taking inventory of her many epithets is not an exercise in cataloging but an indication that Guadalupe has many symbolic meanings, each one arising from a special response to her function in the religious framework of devotees. One of the key factors in the evolution of her extended reign as Mother of the Americas is this multiplicity of votive identifications."

Perhaps because Our Lady of Guadalupe combines spiritual myth with physical evidence, she appeals to a greater mass of people. Even in this country, people from all races and even religions seem attracted to her striking image and compelling story.

The Spanish Virgin of Guadalupe

Our Lady of Guadalupe made her appearance in Mexico in the sixteenth century, but according to Jacqueline Orsini Dunnington, there is evidence of

Spanish worship of Our Lady of Guadalupe three hundred years earlier. The Spanish shrine is located in the town of Cáceres in the Sierra de las Villuercas of the Extremadura region in western Spain and was governed by Jeronymite monks after 1389. This happened to be the hometown of Spanish conquistador Hernán Cortés, who orchestrated the downfall of the Aztec empire and who, ironically, was himself devoted to the Spanish Virgin.

Considered proof of the existence of the mother of Christ, most of the stories attached to sightings of the Virgin Mary take place in isolated areas and send a gentle and spiritual message of the Virgin's love and assistance to the poor and powerless. In the case of the Spanish Virgin, she is said to have appeared to a cowherd. She requested that he dig in a certain spot and build a shrine in her honor at a site that would be revealed to him by her image. Eventually, the cowherd and other townsmen found the site after digging at a tomb, where they discovered a statue of the Virgin. The shrine was built, and the cowherd's son, who had died the year before, was resurrected by the Iberian Virgin Mary of Guadalupe.

The name Guadalupe is traced to an Arabic root, rather than the hypothesized Náhuatl root, which would give the credit for her name to the Aztecs. The root *guad* can be traced to the Moorish-Arabic word *wadi*, which means "ravine through which water flows over a banked river." This describes the location of the area in Cáceres where the Virgin was spotted. The root was used to name several areas in Spain's mountainous region, such as Guadalajara, Guadalquivir, and Guadiana.

Today, this Virgin, whose shrine is still located in Extremadura, is known as the reigning Virgin of Spain and carries a name that reveals this high honor: Nuestra Señora de Guadalupe, La Virgen de la Villuercas, Reina de la Hispanidad, and Patrona de Extremadura (Our Lady of Guadalupe, the Virgen of Villuercas, Queen of the Spanish People, and Patroness of Extremadura). The statue created in her image is much more ostentatious than that of the Mexican Virgin. The Spanish version holds a scepter and wears a miniature jeweled crown, a gold embroidered robe, and a golden halo. In another interesting irony, she is credited for assisting Columbus in the great error in navigation that led him to the New World.

Tonantzin, Mother of the Gods

In Mexico, the Virgin's appearance was associated with the turbulent social situation existing throughout the country. The Spanish conquest had begun, and in 1493 Pope Alexander IV, in a document called the *patronata real,* granted Spain the right to convert all the indigenous peoples to Christianity. Fifteen years later, Spain received the authority to control all missionary activities in the new territories, creating a union rather than a separation of church and state.

In some cases, missionaries took an interest in their new converts and learned more about them, even how to speak their language. The world of Aztec deities included goddesses as well as gods. One goddess, Tonantzin, was the mother of all gods. The shrine of the Virgin of Guadalupe was built on a hill, Tepeyac, which was also the site designated by the Aztecs for Tonantzin worship. This coincidence has led to the theory that Mexicans adopted the Virgin of Guadalupe as a substitute for Tonantzin. In her book *Massacre of the Dreamers* (University of New Mexico Press: Albuquerque, 1994), Ana Castillo writes, "Speculation may be that converting the mother goddess, Tonantzin, into the Virgin Mary as Guadalupe, the brown Virgin, was the Mexic Amerindian [Mexican] people's way of attempting to hold on to their own beliefs. . . . Guadalupe's appearance is seen as a divine blessing on *la raza* [the people] and thus, her banner has led revolutions for freedom and justice."

As the Spanish conquest took root, the Spanish missionaries translated directly into Spanish each Aztec codex (ancient manuscript) they encountered. It was friar Bernardino de Sahagún who first speculated on the history of Aztec worship of Tonantzin and postulated that the natives had supplanted this goddess.

In a paper written in 1576, he revealed his suspicion that the veneration of the Virgin of Guadalupe represented renascent idolatry. Sahagún made the connection between the site, Tepeyac, where the shrine of Our Lady of Guadalupe was built, and the hill where an Aztec temple devoted to the worship of Tonantzin once stood. In what is considered a definitive book on the subject of the Virgin, *Our Lady of Guadalupe: The Origins and Sources of a Mexican National Symbol* (The University of Arizona Press: Tucson, 1995) author Stafford Poole reprints a section of the friar's summary. "Now that the church of Our Lady of Guadalupe has been built there (Tepeyac), they also call her Tonantzin. What may be the basis for this use of Tonantzin is not clear. . . . This appears to be an invention of the devil to cover over idolatry under the ambiguity of this name Tonantzin. They now come to visit this Tonantzin from far away, as far as in former times. The devotion itself is suspect because everywhere there are many churches to Our Lady and they do not go to them. They come from distant lands to this Tonantzin, as they did in former times."

Tonantzin was problematic for the Church as the precursor to Guadalupe because of her less-than-gentle disposition. A fertility deity, Tonantzin was believed to rule the rain and lunar cycles, and because of the importance these powers had over agriculture, blood sacrifices were offered to the goddess. According to Dunnington: "The powers and attributes assigned by the Aztecs to Tonantzin or to a sister goddess encompassed a full range of opposites: the earthly and the cosmic, the creative and the destructive. A menacing goddess is incongruent with the pacific nature of Guadalupe. Indeed, Tonantzin's benevolent female attributes were held in check by her ferocity."

Scholars still disagree over whether the Aztecs replaced Tonantzin with Our Lady of Guadalupe, but there is little disagreement over the story of Guadalupe's appearance being started by the natives. After all, it was one of them to whom she chose to appear.

Prayer to the Virgin

Non-Catholics attend Mass on December 12 to celebrate the Virgin of Guadalupe. Still, many non-Catholics do find her image compelling and have adorned their houses with it. To appreciate the Virgen de Guadalupe, however, is to know her story. She has represented compassion and love to a country that has seen much unrest and suffering, beginning with its initial conquest. The fact that she appeared to a recently converted Indian, that she spoke to him in his native language, and that her image reflects the *mestizaje* (mixing of races) is culturally important. To people of all faiths and all economic conditions, the Virgin of Guadalupe offers hope. Here is a prayer to offer to the Virgen de Guadalupe, to be given in gratitude and with love.

Virgen de Guadalupe
Virgen Morena,
Madre de Salvador,
eres la Reina
de mi linda canción.
Gracias te damos
al dignarte escoger
a nuestro suelo
para morar en él.
Gracias te damos,
gracias por tu bondad.
México entero
hoy se rinde
a tus pies.
Entre las rosas

tu imagen se grabó
en esa tilma
que veneramos hoy.
Virgen sin mancha,
Virgen de Guadalupe,
tu nombre es gozo,
eres toda bondad.
Entre las rosas . . .

DECEMBER 25

¡FELIZ NAVIDAD!

Latinos Celebrate Unique Christmas Traditions

THE MOST irresistible holiday in Christian society must be Christmas. In the United States, this holiday has eclipsed all others in visibility, profitability, and appeal. Not everyone joins in a Saint Patrick's Day celebration, and even Easter gets passed up occasionally, but Christian families—and even many non-Christian ones—don't let Christmas pass without buying gifts, stringing lights, decorating trees, or hanging stockings.

PERENNIAL POINSETTIAS

In Mexico, the Aztecs, who called it Cuetlaxóchitl, appreciated the poinsettia. It became known as *la flor de nochebuena*, or the flower of Christmas Eve. The U.S. name comes from Joel R. Poinsett, a statesman, amateur botanist, and first U.S. Minister to Mexico, who brought back samples of the plant in 1829. Native to the Mexican desert and Central America, the plants did not adapt well to the climate in Poinsett's home state of South Carolina. A century later another man, Paul Ecke, a Los Angeles farmer, began to cultivate the poinsettia as a potted plant.

How did the poinsettia become the official Christmas flower? Some say Franciscan monks gave it that distinction back in the seventeenth century. Others claim a poor Mexican girl, who wished to take flowers to church for Christmas but couldn't afford them, prayed for help. An angel appeared to her and instructed her to gather weeds and take them as an offering. As she approached the church, the weeds were transformed into poinsettias. But according to writer Matthew Holm, "The true story of how the poinsettia became a Christmas flower is only romantic in retrospect. . . . Paul Ecke traveled across the country, promoting and selling his plants, convincing growers, wholesalers, retailers, and ultimately flower lovers that the poinsettia was a great gift and colorful decorating idea for the Christmas season."

Marketing hype notwithstanding, Christmas has retained some of its original goodwill. From third cousins to non-profit organizations, everyone benefits from the spirit of giving that permeates this season. Families also grow closer during this holiday, participating in group activities like tree decorating, caroling, or cookie making. Christmas brings out family traditions with a vengeance, and so it is with Hispanic families. These traditions vary greatly from family to family. The three largest groups in the United States Hispanic community—Puerto Ricans, Mexican Americans, and Cuban Americans—celebrate unique versions of the Christmas tradition.

Good Night, Noche Buena

Like many Latino customs, *la navidad* has been modified over time by American traditions, and for Cuban Americans, who depend on older generations to be the keepers of tradition, the loss has been keenly felt. In *Las Christmas*, a collection of Christmas memories from different Latino authors, Gustavo Pérez Firmat compares the Cuban Christmases of his past to the current celebrations his family shares with relatives in Miami.

In Cuba, before the revolution, he remembers, *nochebuena* was the adult event, while the Epiphany was for children. The children received no presents on December 25, but did on January 6. His family had already adopted the Western custom of decorating a Christmas tree, even though fir trees were few and far between in Cuba. The families would fast before attending midnight Mass and the children would have to take naps in order to be rested for church. After Mass, the party began, with rum drinks and rumba dancing.

In the United States, that schedule of events was a little harder to maintain, even

Christmas may have its requisite commercial elements, but it's still a Christian holiday with religious roots. For Latinos, traditions like Christmas Mass and nativity scenes with Jesus, Mary, Joseph, the shepherds, and three kings are especially important. Of course, intertwined with the commercial and spiritual aspects of Christmas are the individual family traditions.

Latino Christmases tend to focus on the spiritual side of the holiday. To begin with, Christmas has several names in Spanish: *la navidad, las navidades,* or *las pascuas.* The celebration usually begins with Advent and reaches a climax on *nochebuena,* or Christmas Eve, with families attending midnight Mass, or *misa de gallo.* From the religious reenactment of the pilgrimage of Mary and Joseph through Jerusalem in search of shelter called a *posada,* to the caroling marathon celebrated in Puerto Rico called the *asalto navideño*, or *parranda,* religion reigns supreme in Hispanic celebrations.

Food is also an essential and universal Christmas element. Even in this image-conscious country, many people accept the weight gain and forget about diets in order to savor the holiday. Hispanic families prepare delectable traditional holiday fare without which Christmas would feel like just another day. Mexican American families may cook *tamales,* Puerto Ricans have a similar dish, *pasteles puertorriqueños,* that gives a tropical twist to the same recipe, and Cuban American families spend the day perfecting their holi-

day entrée, *lechón asado*. As more and more generations of Latinos settle in the United States, the need to
perpetuate these customs increases.

Christmas in the Caribbean

In Cuba and Puerto Rico, the Christmas season is still
celebrated more on January 6 than on December 25.
In Cuba, Christmas has reemerged as a holiday only
recently because Communist dictator Fidel Castro had
banned the holiday for years. Houses could not be decorated nor gifts exchanged during the season. The
only tradition that remained there was midnight Mass,
and even this was attended secretly. According to
Charito Calvachi Wakefield, author of *Navidad
Latinoamericana/Latin American Christmas* (Latin
American Creations Publishing: Lancaster, Pennsylvania,
1997), "The Christmas traditions in Cuba survived
only two years after the revolution in 1959. When the Marxist system was
implanted, all the roots of Christmas traditions were destroyed. . . . For the
majority of people [in Cuba], Christmas is just another day."

after more family members followed from
Cuba to settle in the States. Older generations continued to try to re-create the
traditional celebrations in Cuba that
focused on *nochebuena*, while their children naturally focused on what was popular in this country, Santa Claus and
Christmas Day. Writes Firmat: "The older
Cubans, mostly men like my father and my
uncles, celebrated *nochebuena*; their
American-born grandchildren did the
same for Christmas. . . . During these
balanced years, the prospect of
Christmas morning made *nochebuena* a
little more sedate, and *nochebuena* made
Christmas a little more lively."

The pull of such an important holiday could not be forever hidden. Despite
governmental pressure, many Cubans continued to practice their Catholic
faith, and in 1998, a desire of its adherents was finally realized. In 1997, Pope
John Paul II announced plans to visit Cuba, marking the first time since
Castro's takeover and dissolution of the Cuban Catholic Church that a pope
would set foot on the island. Economic and global pressures had caught up
with the enigmatic dictator, and the country made plans to welcome the Pope
enthusiastically. After Pope John Paul II's historic trip to Cuba in January

1998, the government reversed its position and the first public Christmas concert was held in Havana in December of that year.

In the United States, Cuban Americans approach the holiday in the usual way, with Christmas lights, trees, nativity scenes, and family gatherings. In fact, due to the island's closeness to the United States, many American or "Western" traditions like Santa Claus and Christmas trees had already been adopted in Cuba. Christmas Eve is the focal point of the holiday for Cuban Americans, although some families also celebrate the Epiphany on January 6. On Christmas Eve, the family gathers for a traditional dinner and then socializes until it's time to go to midnight Mass. "At my family's home [on Christmas Eve] in Miami's "Little Havana,' all my relatives will gather Friday to eat, exchange gifts, and tell old stories," writes Miguel Perez in an article published in *The Record,* a New Jersey paper. "With several American-born additions to our family sitting on their laps, they will celebrate like we did in Cuba—listening to Spanish carols, covering a Christmas tree with twinkling lights and glittering tinsel, and setting up a *nacimiento* (nativity scene) that reminds us of the real meaning of Christmas."

Puerto Rican Parrandas

The most unique Christmas celebration in Puerto Rico is a caroling block party called *asaltos navideños*, or *parrandas*. The caroling can take place throughout the Christmas season, starting at the beginning of Advent and sometimes lasting past the Epiphany. The two most ambitious nights for *parrandas*, however, are Christmas Eve and the Epiphany, when the singing can go on through the night and into the early morning. *Parrandas* begin with one family going over to their neighbor's house without warning; hence the name *asalto* (assault). The revelers sing *aguinaldos*, a traditional Puerto Rican Christmas carol noted for its six-syllable verse line. They may also be accompanied by musicians playing traditional instruments like the *güiro* (made from a gourd), the triangle, and *maracas*. For their singing and playing efforts, revelers are invited inside the house to eat such traditional holiday treats as rice with coconut, papaya sweets, crullers (donuts), marzipan, and nougat from Spain.

Then the hosts join the carolers, who move on to the next house, where again they are invited inside for more food and beverages. Instead of champagne, traditional alcoholic drinks are served, like *ponche* and *coquito* (Puerto Rican eggnog) as well as rum and beer. The caroling and eating continue to the next block and usually through the night, stretching into the next day. Inhabitants are often awakened from their beds to the sound of the carolers on their doorstep. The final stop on the *parranda* may be the only one that is predetermined, since the singers may not arrive until early morning. Ideally, the festivities will end with breakfast or the traditional *sopón,* a thick chicken and rice stew, at the final stop on the following day.

In *The Puerto Ricans' Spirit* author María Teresa Babín writes: "In our lexicon, there exists the verb, *reyar* . . . the custom of gathering together a group of revelers to descend upon a neighbor, at whose door one sang a typical song or carol, was followed in towns and in the country, and persists today, although it is less common than previously." This practice is more widespread in Puerto Rico than in the United States, but the importance of Christmas carols, including *"El Asalto,"* the song sung by revelers to announce themselves, endures.

TRADITIONAL *LUMINARIAS*

The custom of *luminarias* began in New Mexico with Native Americans, who adapted the bonfire celebration to suit Christmas. Instead of a huge bonfire, they placed little fires outside of churches and pueblos. When Chinese paper lanterns began to arrive in the area in the beginning of the nineteenth century, *luminarias* were placed in paper bags. Today, mass-produced outdoor decorations—plastic "bags" on electric light strings—are available, but in New Mexico, the tradition of filling half the bag with sand, to make it stable, and then placing a lit candle inside, is still practiced. It's easy to make this traditional Christmas lantern. The trick is to use enough sand in the bag to open it completely and allow the candles to be firmly affixed and not blow over. Follow these simple directions:

1. **Use standard brown paper lunch bags. Open each bag and put about a cup of sand in the bottom of the bag.**

2. **Place the bags every two to three feet along the curbside, driveway, or path you wish to decorate.**

3. **Center small votive candles in the bottom of each bag, adding a little more sand to be sure the candle has a firm footing.**

4. **Light with a long match or lighter at twilight, and enjoy!**

Mexican American Influences

Many Mexican customs such as *tamales*, poinsettias, and *luminarias* have already crossed over into this country and been adopted as North American Christmas traditions. Poinsettias (originally used by the Aztecs and later called *la flor de nochebuena*) have become an American institution. Although their takeover has not yet been as complete as the poinsettia's, *luminarias* (lit candles in paper bags partially filled with sand) have definitely become a Christmas tradition in the Southwest, where they were born. Rows of *luminarias* along paths, sidewalks, and streets symbolically light the way for the Christmas *posada*—Mary and Joseph's journey to Bethlehem. In fact, the city of Albuquerque holds an annual *luminaria* event on Christmas Eve called the

Sun Tran Christmas Luminaria Tour, which takes participants on buses along a route with homes and business that feature *luminarias*.

Another important Christmas symbol, the nativity, takes on a central role in all Latino households. For Cuban and Puerto Rican families, arranging the *nacimiento* or *pesebres* (manger) is an integral Christmas Eve ritual. Besides arranging a nativity, the traditional Mexican American application of the nativity involves the story of Mary and Joseph's journey to find shelter. This story had such a great significance in Mexican culture that it produced two events: the *posada* and *La Pastorela*.

A *posada* is a short parade or pilgrimage that reenacts Mary and Joseph's journey to Bethlehem and their struggle to find shelter. It's usually organized by individual churches located in the heart of Latino neighborhoods. In Mexico, where the tradition originated, families participate in *posadas* throughout Advent from December 16 through 24. Like so many Mexican customs, the *posada* combines indigenous and Christian rituals.

"History shows that when the Spanish friars accompanying the conquistadors tried to convert the Mexican Indians to Catholicism, they found the task easier when they incorporated a key element of the Indian's belief system: reenactment," writes Mercedes Olivera in a December 17, 1997, article in the *Dallas Morning News*. According to Olivera, the *posada* survives today practically in its original form, "when the friars divided the Indian congregation into *peregrinos,* or pilgrims, and *posaderos,* or innkeepers."

In the United States, the procession usually takes place just once, but like the Mexican procession, the *posada* includes children and adults carrying candles, who walk behind the figures of Mary and Joseph or individuals portraying them. Animals, such as sheep, donkeys, and even camels if they can be found, are also often included. Set on a prearranged route, the procession takes participants to designated sites, usually houses, where the *peregrinos* sing a song requesting shelter. The procession then reaches its final destination, where Mary and Joseph are accepted. Once that ritual is performed, the party begins. Food and drinks, usually something simple like candies, *pan dulce* (sweet bread), and hot chocolate, are served to the celebrants while musicians play traditional songs.

Similar to the *posada* is *La Pastorela*. Both are set against the backdrop of the birth of Jesus, but *La Pastorela* is a play rather than a procession. The play recounts another journey to Bethlehem, that of the three shepherds; hence the name *La Pastorela* (Shepherds' Story). In the story, the shepherds begin their journey lightheartedly, singing songs in anticipation of seeing the Christ child, whose arrival has been foretold to them by Saint Michael. Along the way, they encounter other travelers, beginning with a wise hermit who decides to join the group. Their next encounter is more ominous. The devil, Luzbel, hopes to stop the shepherds on their pilgrimage and sends his demons to do this. They tempt the *pastores* with money and sex, and when that doesn't work, the devil turns them into sheep. Saint Michael appears in the end to battle with the devil to save the shepherds. He defeats Luzbel and sends him back to Hell. The play ends as the shepherds reach their destination to behold the Christ child.

La Pastorela offers parents an entertaining opportunity both to reaffirm the culture and also to impress upon children a moral for living and the true meaning of Christmas.

Latino Holiday Fare

No holiday pulls at the heartstrings like Christmas, which is one reason it has become one of the most important holidays in this country. The holiday's appeal starts with its message of hope and love, which manifests itself each year when families gather to celebrate the season. An essential element of the holiday is food. Christmas is not only special, it's delicious.

Every family guards its own holiday recipes, and traditional Christmas cuisine is also an integral part of the holiday celebration. Many Latino families have adopted the American Christmas Day menu of turkey, dressing, mashed potatoes, cranberry sauce, and pumpkin pie, but throughout the holiday, and on the all-important Noche Buena, traditional holiday foods abound.

Masa for la Raza

Mexican American families proudly combine their American and Mexican roots at Christmas. Many families will cook the obligatory turkey, but they will also prepare (some may prefer to buy them) the Mexican traditional holiday meal of *tamales*, rice, and beans. The *tamales* are usually prepared weeks in advance—and by the dozens—in a group effort called a *tamalada*. The *tamalada* usually involves relatives and friends who converge on one house to lend a hand in the *tamale* production. For their work, each helper usually receives a dozen or two of the *tamales*.

The *tamale* has ancient roots, dating back to the Aztecs in the thirteenth century. Its original name was *tamalli*, which means "patty" or "cake." In *Flavors of Mexico*, author Marlena Spieler writes, "Tamales were served by the Aztecs, Mayans, and other Indian nations and were greatly enhanced by the Spanish introduction of pork and cooking fat."

Considering its simple ingredients, corn meal *masa* and shredded pork stuffed in a corn shuck, this little morsel is a labor of love. The steps in the process include preparing the meat, cleaning the shucks, kneading the *masa* until it floats, *embarando* (spreading the *masa* on the shuck), adding the meat, folding the shuck closed, sealing in the meat and *masa,* and standing them upright in a pot so that they can steam to cook.

Like poinsettias, *tamales* are quickly crossing over to become a Christmas tradition in many homes. In Dallas, Texas, Mexican restaurants and tortilla factories scramble each year to meet the demand for *tamale* and *masa* orders. In a December 25, 1998, article in the *Dallas Morning News,* Jesse Moreno, owner of La Popular Tamale House in East Dallas, tells of how he sacrificed a peaceful holiday to keep his customers happy. "I was up here making *tamales* until midnight last night and was back again at five o'clock. People just expect it, to be able to eat *tamales* at Christmas, and we can't disappoint them."

Many families make efforts to pass on the tradition. Recipes have also been modified to include chicken rather than beef, or vegetarian versions with just beans and cheese, to appeal to more health-conscious palates. Even sugar *tamales* have emerged. "It's just a part of Christmas," says Moreno. "[It's] a tradition that means a lot to us. The main reason I'm doing this, it certainly isn't for the money, it's for my sons. I want them to know this tradition."

Pass the *Pasteles*

Puerto Rican families prepare a dish similar to the *tamale* but with Caribbean variations. Called *pasteles* after the paste (corollary to the *masa* in tamales) that surrounds the stuffing, these morsels follow much of the same procedure as the *tamalada,* with just a few changes to the recipe. Rather than corn shucks, the *pasteles* are encased in plantain leaves and tied. They're also stuffed with a variety of concoctions: pork, ground meat, black beans, fruits, and nuts. The meat stuffing may also include green or black olives, or raisins. Pasteles also tend to be flatter than tamales, due to the larger packaging of the plantain leaf over the corn shuck, and they're boiled, not steamed.

Other savory ingredients of the Puerto Rican Christmas meal include suckling pig, rice and green pigeon peas, and goat or veal stew. When the traditional turkey meal is prepared, it has variations like stuffing made of ground meat and vegetables. Preparing *pasteles* also brings families together to produce these labor-intensive delicacies. According to chef Oswald Rivera in *Puerto Rican Cuisine in America: Nuyorican and Bodega Recipes*, "To be honest, preparing *pasteles* is a pain because it's so time consuming. A food proces-

A Christmas Carol

There are many Latino Christmas carols, such as "Las Posadas" or "Llegaron ya Los Reyes," but in the United States, the Christmas carol that has successfully crossed over into Spanish is "Silent Night" (translated as "Noche de Paz"). The melody is already familiar to almost everyone, so here are the lyrics to the song for those who would like to sing it in Spanish.

NOCHE DE PAZ

Noche de paz, noche de amor
todo duerme en derredor
Entre los astros que esparcen su
    luz
bella anunciando al Niñito Jesús,
brilla la estrella de paz.
Brilla la estrella de paz.

Noche de paz, noche de amor
ved qué bello resplandor
luce en el rostor del Niño Jesús,
en el pesebre del mundo la luz,
astro de eterno fulgor.
astro de eterno fulgor.

sor helps. There are still those who prefer to make them the old-fashioned way by grating all the ingredients by hand. Among these include my father and Uncle Carlos. Tradition is tradition. I prefer the shortcuts. Either way, *pasteles* is a project, not a quick fix."

Puerto Ricans prepare a Christmas eggnog with a twist called *coquito*. The key ingredients are dark rum, sweetened condensed milk, evaporated milk, egg yolks, and coconut. "In Puerto Rican neighborhoods, the *coquito* flows during the Las Fiestas Patronales, or the Feast of the Patron Saints, and Christmas," writes Rivera. "Every family has its own recipe. According to my elders, in olden times the success of a shindig was measured on the quality of the family *coquito*."

A Cuban Christmas Feast

Cattle and turkeys were in short supply in the Caribbean, but thanks to the Spaniards, pork was not. Therefore, a Christmas celebration in Puerto Rican or Cuban American households will feature *lechón asado*, which is roasted pork, usually a suckling pig. For Cubans, this tradition compares to family cooking projects like the *tamalada* or the Puerto Rican *pasteles*.

In Cuba and in some parts of Miami where families have a large enough backyard, the *lechón asado* process starts by digging a *púa* (a rectangular hole in the ground) to roast the pig. A pole that runs through the pig helps suspend the *lechón* over a fire, to which is added guava leaves for flavor. Basting the pig is equally essential. "The ingredient that gives Cuban-style suckling pig its special flavor is bitter orange. Lemon, lime, or orange juice can be substituted in this recipe, but bitter orange will give the pig a distinct and superior flavor," writes Linette Creen in *A Taste of Cuba*. The operation begins in the morning with family members taking turns rotating the pig. By the afternoon, the workers are served Spanish wine, so by the evening when the pig is done, the party mood is in full swing.

Noche de paz, noche de amor,
llena el cielo de resplandor,
en las alturas resuena un cantar:
"os anuncio una dicha sin par,
en la tierra ha nacido Dios,
hoy en Belén de Judá.

Because of the work involved in the preparation of *lechón asado,* the cooking component of the tradition has faded, especially for Cuban Americans in Miami, although the meat is still served. "This was very much a country tradition," says Carlos Verdecia, editor of *Hispanic* magazine. "Even in Havana, many people would prepare the pork and then take it to a baker to cook since he had a large enough oven. That's pretty much how it's handled in Miami." For families who lack the yard but still want to cook the pork themselves, Verdecia says Miamians have invented a gadget called the *caja china* (Chinese box) in which the pork is placed and then flipped periodically, over an open fire.

Besides roasted pork, many Cuban meals include black beans, white rice or *congrí* (a bean and rice casserole), fried plantains, Cuban bread, and confections like Spanish marzipan. One of the more traditional desserts is the *turrón* (nougat), which can be prepared in a variety of ways, depending on the nuts used. *Alicante's turrón* features a very hard nut, the *alicante,* while *jijona's turrón* turns out more like cake than candy and features the softer *jijona* nut. There is also a *turrón* made with almonds and *membrillo* (quince). These Spanish sweets tend to be bought in grocery stores rather than homemade, much like fruit bread. In Calvachi Wakefield's book, *Navidad*

Latinoamericana, the Cuban feast, before Castro interrupted it, reflected the abundance of fruits and nuts found on the island. "Common foods were eaten . . . nuts and *avellanas* (hazelnuts) were a favorite part of the meal. . . . Dinner would be served at 9 P.M. and the meal concluded with everyone drinking wine. After dinner, everyone attended the Misa de Gallo (midnight Mass)."

From *luminarias* to *lechón asado,* Latino Christmas traditions reflect history, geography, and spirituality. Some traditions have already been incorporated into the mainstream celebration of Christmas, like poinsettias. Other traditions, particularly feast dishes, may seem more difficult to incorporate. For the true adventurer, cookbooks can provide recipes, but attending a *posada* or joining a *parranda* can only add to an already special holiday.

DÍA DE LOS REYES

Reclaiming the Epiphany

CHRISTMAS HAS almost completely eclipsed the Epiphany in the United States. Because our society tends to focus on the great exchange of gifts on Christmas, the Epiphany has all but disappeared. The buildup to December 25 can begin as early as Labor Day in some shopping malls. The Christmas industry is so organized that for three to four months out of the year, very little can compete. Even Halloween and Thanksgiving become mere milestones to the big event in December. The marketing effort is so exhaustive, however, that sometimes when the day arrives, it can be anticlimactic. Once the holiday season is over, only after-Christmas sales and New Year's Eve remain to look forward to.

But not so in many Latino households. For these families, who remain connected to all the events of the religious season, Christmas is not an anticlimax. Nor does it signal the end of the holiday season. It is merely the high point in a vigil that begins in late November, with the start of Advent, and ends on January 6.

Over the centuries, Latinos, especially Puerto Rican and Cuban families, have maintained the celebration of the Epiphany, or El Día de los Reyes. In Puerto Rico the day plays such an important part of the holiday celebration that it's considered a national holiday with a special focus on children. A second, more substantial, round of gifts is distributed on this day, symbolizing the gifts given to the infant Jesus by the three kings, or magi.

Cubans also recognize the Epiphany, but before that date, they practice an interesting New Year's Eve tradition: they eat twelve grapes, one for every stroke of midnight. Passed down from the Spanish, it's a unique version of the New Year's resolution.

The New Year brings a common experience of symbolic and real opportunities for a new beginning. Whether it's extending the holiday mood to include the Epiphany or toasting the New Year with grapes as well as champagne, these Hispanic traditions ease the transition from post-holiday blahs and instill new energy for the year to come.

Shoebox of Dreams

Día de los Reyes is a holiday for children. For Latino children, the basic ritual of the Three Kings is the shoebox filled with grass for the camels. Children can choose any shoebox and can even decorate it specifically for Christmas and reuse it each year. A letter to the Three Kings, modeled after letters to Santa, can be attached, and a bowl or cans of water can also be left behind for the camels. Like the bites taken out of Santa's cookies and the empty glass of milk, which prove he was there, the Three Kings and their camels should leave their mark with missing grass and water—certainly at the homes of good children, anyway! *Feliz día de los reyes magos.*

THE GRAPE TOAST

Streamers, firecrackers, bells, whistles, and a champagne toast have traditionally welcomed the New Year in the United States, but in Miami Cuban Americans celebrate with something unexpected: grapes. The origin of the tradition probably traces back to Spain, where it is also performed as a New Year's tradition. This tradition is not exclusively limited to Cuban Americans, but it is performed more consistently in this community. The reason that Cuban Americans embraced this tradition is more obvious than it may appear. "Cuba is the most Spanish of all of Latin America," says Lisandro Pérez, sociology professor at Florida International University in Miami. "Spain was in control there [and Puerto Rico] the longest, until 1898, and you have many Cubans who are first- and second-generation Spanish descendants there." Like the grape toast, many other Spanish customs hold great interest for Cuban Americans and are still perpetuated, sometimes exclusively, by this community.

The origin of the grape toast itself is less clear. Although it appears to be Spanish, others theorize that it was taken from a Roman tradition associated with Bacchus. José Zavada, executive vice president of Hiram Walker in Mexico City and a native of Spain, theorizes that the grape toast is related to wine and the revelry of Bacchus, the god of wine. "In the tradition of the bacchanals, which were held to bring luck and a good harvest, I believe the grape toast was born out of the same intention," says Zavada.

The custom goes like this: Near the stroke of midnight, family members collect their glasses and fill them with twelve grapes. The number of grapes signifies the twelve months in the year that has passed and the twelve months in the year yet to come. At the stroke of midnight, everyone toasts with a *"¡Salud!"* and eats the grapes, ideally before the clock strikes 12:01 A.M. "I remember it was very important, especially to the older folks, to eat the grapes quickly, for good luck," says Pérez.

Toasting the New Year is a wish for good luck in the year to come. Making New Year's resolutions expands the desire for a prosperous new year by adding goals. The noisy New Year's Eve tradition that involves streamers, bells, and whistles was borrowed from birthday celebrations symbolically welcoming the New Year baby—and champagne just completes the party atmosphere. Celebrating the New Year is all about adding luck, positive energy, and good karma to the year to come, so adding another element, like a grape toast, only increases the positive vibe.

A Divine Sighting

In Europe, January 6 has pagan roots. In pre-Christian Britain, a January 6 celebration marked the first sunny days of winter when farmers could begin to prepare their fields for spring planting. A pagan party, called the feast of the Epiphany, was marked by loud singing (to wake up sleeping trees and vegetation) and drinking of a strongly fermented ale called wassail. William Shakespeare commemorated this pagan festival in his play *Twelfth Night.*

The Christian interpretation of January 6 shares the pagan need for celebration, although with a little less zeal. The Epiphany marks the arrival of the three wise men (or the three kings)—Melchior, Gaspar, and Baltazar—into Bethlehem to view the Christ child and to offer gifts of gold, frankincense, and myrrh. In the early days of Christianity, the date of the sighting held more significance than the date of Jesus's birth.

The concept of the Twelfth Day of Christmas is not a new one. Christian civilizations have recognized it for centuries. In the Greek Orthodox Church, the Epiphany is celebrated on the same date and is considered one of its most sacred feast days. But the Eastern Orthodox Church has simply maintained the importance of an event that used to matter in Western Christian communities. The celebration of the Epiphany retained its importance up until the dawn of the twentieth century.

In a 1938 article in *The Ecclesiastical Review,* Dom Albert Hammenstede lamented the early signs that the celebration was fading. "Christmastide, considered from the liturgical point of view, has two summits: Christmas day, on 25 December, and epiphany, on 6 January," he wrote. "The latter feast is older than the former and, historically considered in the light of the earlier Christian ages, more important. But Christmas, the feast of the Nativity of our Lord, has become nearer and dearer to our hearts, and there is even a danger that in our days epiphany might be undervalued and considered merely as a remembrance of the three Magi who visited the crib of Bethlehem."

The contemporary use of the word "epiphany" means a moment of sudden clarity, and the word also means "the coming or manifestation, especially of a divine being." According to Hammenstede, the word has a much more sacred origin. Its root is actually the Greek word *epiphania* and was used to describe the momentous act by the king or emperor of presenting himself to the people. Because rulers were considered quasidivine, their public appearance was a peek not at the ruler himself but at the divinity he held inside him. "From this we gather that Christ's epiphany means the solemn and visible coming of Him who as God-King had been hidden from all eternity and whose visible manifestation to His creatures one would never have expected," explains Hammenstede.

Besides the appearance of Christ, the Epiphany has three other purposes: to provide a moment for the adoration of Christ as a manifestation of God, to appreciate him as a representation of the human race, and to recognize him as the redeemer. This four-pointed purpose to the epiphany gives it equal—or even greater—religious significance than Easter. Taking from the Greek root of the celebration, Hammenstede explained: "For them [Greeks] the death and resurrection of Christ was the marriage between Christ and His Church as the epiphany of Christ was the betrothal. . . . Now we understand that the season of Advent is in the first place a preparation for Epiphany and not Christmas Day."

Like the Epiphany, Christmas has a pagan origin that traces back to the Romans, who celebrated December 25 as the feast of the *sol invictus* (invisible sun). The date was the winter solstice, at which time the sun, which was personified by the Romans, seemed to regain strength, reenergizing for the next year. "Now Christ is the light, the spiritual and divine sun of the world," asserts Hammenstede. "So it was natural for the earlier Christians to claim the twenty-fifth of December as Christ's birthday, for He is the true Light that enlightens every man who comes into the world."

Considering the innate significance of the Epiphany and the fact that both Christmas and the Epiphany evolved to include gift giving, the switch to elevate December 25 over January 6 is related to their symbolism. The Epiphany celebrates the divinity of Christ, whereas Christmas celebrates his humanity. In the West it is his humanity that impresses followers, who take comfort in the concept of a divine human who was capable of human weaknesses. "The Eastern Way is a royal one," writes Hammenstede. "It proclaims the primacy of the Logos over the Ethos, of grace over nature.... On the other hand, how lovely and full of charm is Christmas Day.... The King of Heaven took upon Himself a real human body! By His human nature He has become our brother according to the flesh and our most faithful friend in all our earthly struggles."

Latinos and the Epiphany

According to a *Dallas Morning News* article published January 6, 1999, there is a growing effort in England to revive the Twelfth Day of Christmas celebration. In a country where sixty percent of the population does not attend church, the Epiphany is seen as a means of getting people to reembrace religion. That's not necessary in Latino societies. For them, the Epiphany is more meaningful than Christmas, and that message was delivered to the indigenous people by the priests in the sixteenth century. Obviously, it was not forgotten. Celebrated from Spain to the Dominican Republic, the Epiphany remains an important holiday tradition. Among United States Latinos, however, the tradition is waning, with mainly Puerto Ricans enthusiastically upholding the holiday.

In Barcelona, men dressed as the magi, Baltazar, Gaspar, and Melchior, sail to the port city on the eve of the Epiphany. Accompanied by a regatta of other boats, some carry candy, which is tossed into the crowd of celebrants, and one boat also contains coal—a reminder to children not to misbehave. In Spanish homes, shoes rather than stockings are placed in the living room, and in the morning, they are found piled with gifts and topped with a sugar treat—a sweeter, gentler reminder than coal. In Mexico, as in Spain, shoes are put out on January 5 and covered with presents while the children sleep. However, in Mexico, the shoe tends to be a *huarache* sandal. Even in the remote town of Sinsinawa, Wisconsin, the Dominican community has established an Epiphany celebration. The Catholic Church there plays a stronger role in this celebration, which is viewed as a moment for "contemplation rather than commerce."

But the Puerto Rican community seems to make the most out of the Epiphany. According to María Teresa Babín, author of *The Puerto Ricans' Spirit: Their History, Life, and Culture*, "The day of the Magi, and the successive days up to the Octave of Bethlehem (eight days following the Epiphany), held more splendor in the past than they do today—children received their gifts on the morning of the sixth of January . . . the Epiphany was really Christmas on the island."

In Puerto Rico, the celebration of the three kings is a national holiday. All businesses shut down to allow families to mark the holiday. On January 5, children gather grass to symbolically feed the animals ridden by the kings. Rather than shoes, the grass is packed into shoeboxes, which are then left under the bed with the hope that in the morning they will be filled with gifts. "The New Year was received, as in all the Western world, with the typical gaiety of farewell to the Old Year," writes Babín. "But the most beloved part of the celebration in our land was the festival of the Wise Men."

Although the author describes the event as less spectacular than it used to be, twenty-one years after Babín wrote her book, the Epiphany celebration was revived by Puerto Rico Governor Pedro Rossellio. During his term, between 1992 and 2000, Rossellio focused on maintaining the island's cultural past, and an important part of that history included the Feast of the Magi. He worked to find sponsors for the project, and once that was accomplished, Rossellio became a modern-day Santa Claus, Puerto Rican-style. On the Epiphany, Rossellio instigated a nationwide toy giveaway. Children from throughout the island journeyed to its capital, San Juan, to personally receive a gift from the governor. The process took an entire day and lines stretched for miles, but miraculously, patience abounded during the event.

Compared to other communities—except Eastern Orthodox Christians, who still see the Epiphany as an essential event—Puerto Ricans still give the Epiphany the most attention. "The epiphany has suffered in the diaspora," says Manuel Ortiz, a New York-based consultant and native of Juayama, Puerto Rico. "Because of the pressure in this country to celebrate Christmas, the Epiphany is not celebrated with the same scope."

On the island, the Christmas marketing onslaught has not been ignored, but "the real Christmas is still the Epiphany," says Ortiz. Today, children do receive a small gift on December 25, and, not to feel left out, adults also choose to exchange gifts on this day. The main gifts for the children are reserved, however, for the Epiphany. January 6 has become completely focused on the children, says Ortiz. "In Puerto Rico, there is no confusion between the three kings and Santa Claus."

Many Latinos hold fond memories of celebrations of the three kings of long past. In *Las Christmas: Favorite Latino Authors Share Their Holiday Memories* (Alfred A. Knopf: New York, 1998), Puerto Rican author Esmeralda Santiago describes the annual ritual her family performed for the celebration of the three kings. "The night before the three magi were to come, my sisters and brother and I searched for the freshest, most tender blades of grass to leave in our shoes for the Magi's camels. We placed the shoes under our beds, the toes sticking out so that the Magi would see them. . . . I woke up while it was still dark. Two shadows moved around the room carrying bundles in their hands. I closed my eyes quickly. It must be two of the magi, I thought, while the third stays outside with the camels."

There is a celebration in New York City every year, begun in 1976 by El Museo del Barrio, a museum based in the Bronx that focuses on Latino art and culture. The celebration and the museum were started by a group of artists and educators who felt a need to reclaim and institutionalize the holiday for the community, especially the children, says Miriam de Uriarte, curriculum coordinator at the museum. The museum's Three Kings program starts in November, when it offers workshops on making *santos de palo*, a traditional wooden carving of religious figures. The *santos* will become part of a household Christmas celebration, placed with the nativity or separately in a home altar.

The museum works closely with area schools, which also bring the children to visit the museum to view its collection of more than 600 *santos*. As January 6 approaches, the children participate in classes at the museum, where they make crowns, capes, or other costume pieces to wear in the Día de Los Reyes parade. Workshops are also held to make toys that are distributed to the children at the parade. "It all builds up to the parade, where more than 2,500 children will participate," says de Uriarte.

For the parade, three wise men are selected from several community groups to lead it. Musicians ride in a truck, accompanying the children, who march a mile and a half. The procession takes about two hours, ending at the museum. The museum also works with the Bronx Zoo to rent camels and sheep to participate in the parade. The first 600 kids who sign up for the parade are invited into the museum theater, where they receive their gifts.

According to Chiori Santiago in an article in *Latina* magazine, Santa Claus is a very recent invention. He can be dated to approximately 1873, when a poem written by Clement Clarke Moore, "A Visit from St. Nicolas" was published. The concept of gift giving really originated with the three kings, and for families who choose to postpone their gift-giving ritual, celebrating the Epiphany can help overcome the commercialization of December 25 and bring a little more meaning to the gift of giving.

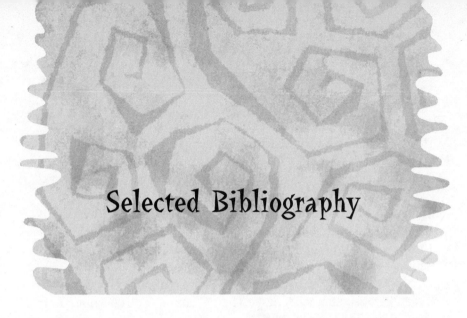

Selected Bibliography

Babín, María Teresa. *The Puerto Ricans' Spirit: Their History, Life, and Culture.* New York: Macmillan Publishing Co., Inc., 1971.

Castillo, Ana. *Massacre of the Dreamers.* Albuquerque: University of New Mexico Press, 1994.

Dunnington, Jacqueline Orsini. *Guadalupe: Our Lady of New Mexico.* Sante Fe: Museum of New Mexico Press, 1999.

Elyjiw, Zenon. "Ukrainian Pysanka: Easter Eggs as Talismans." *The Ukranian Weekly*, 16 April 1995.

Firmat, Gustavo Pérez. "Goodnight to Nochebuena." In *Las Christmas: Favorite Latino Authors Share Their Holiday Memories.* New York: Alfred A. Knopf, 1998.

Francis, Mark and Arturo J. Perez-Rodriguez. *Primero Dios: Hispanic Liturgical Resource.* Chicago: Liturgy Training Publications, 1997.

Gonzalez-Pando, Miguel. *The Cuban Americans.* Westport, Connecticut: Greenwood Press, 1998.

Gutierrez, Hector. " Big Bash on Tap for Columbus Day." *Denver Rocky Mountain News*, 10 October 1997.

Hammenstede, Dom Albert. "Christmas and Epiphany: The Western and the Eastern Way." *The Ecclesiastical Review*, January 1938.

Harvey, Marion. *Mexican Crafts and Craftspeople.* Cranbury, New Jersey: Associated University Presses, 1987.

Krauze, Enrique. *Mexico: Biography of Power*. New York: Harper Collins, 1997.

Martinez, Yleana. "Crackin' Cascarones." *Hispanic*, March 1996.

Meléndez, Father Michael. "The Blessed Virgin Mary, Mother of the Divine Providence Puerto Rico." Flushing, New York: St. Michael's Parish, n.d.

Murgoei, Agness. "Rumanian Easter Eggs." *Folklore* 20 (1909).

The National Institute of Hispanic Liturgy. *Gift and Promise Customs and Traditions in Hispanic Rites of Marriage*. Portland: Oregon Catholic Press, 1997.

Ojito, Mira. "Reason to Celebrate, Twice, for Columbus: Hispanic and Italian Parades Staunchly Stake Their Claim on Fifth Avenue." *New York Times*, 14 October 1996.

Olivera, Mercedes. "Posada Brings to Life Mary and Joseph's Search for Lodging." *Dallas Morning News*, 17 December 1997.

Olson, James, and Olson, Judith. *Cuban Americans: From Trauma to Triumph*. New York: Twayne Publishers, 1995.

Oxford Dictionary of Saints. New York: Oxford University Press, 1981.

Perez, Miguel. "Dreaming of Navidad." *The Record* (Bergen County, New Jersey), 22 December 1993.

Poole, Stafford. *Our Lady of Guadalupe: The Origins and Sources of a Mexican National Symbol*. Tucson: The University of Arizona Press, 1995.

Preet, Edythe. "Ancient Role of Eggs in Religion Still Unbroken." *Washington Times*, 31 March 1999.

Ramirez, Marc. "It's My Party, and I Can Splurge if I Want To." *New Times* (Phoenix, Arizona), 15 June 1994.

Rivera, Oswald. *The Nuyorican Cookbook*. New York: Four Walls Eight Windows, 1993.

Rodriguez, Jeanette. *Our Lady of Guadalupe: Faith and Empowerment among Mexican-American Women*. Austin: University of Texas Press, 1994.

Salcedo, Michele. *Quinceañera*. New York: Henry Holt and Company, 1997.

Santiago, Chiori. "El Día de los Reyes." *Latina*, December 1997.

Santiago, Esmerelda. "A Baby Doll Like My Cousin Jenny's." In *Las Christmas: Favorite Latino Authors Share Their Holiday Memories.* New York: Alfred A. Knopf, 1998.

Sommers, Laurie Kay. "Symbol and Style in Cinco de Mayo." *Journal of American Folklore* 98, no. 390 (1995).

South East Pastoral Institute (SEPI). "Las Avocaciones Marianas en la Religiosidad Popular Latinoamericana." *Documentaciones Sureste*, February 1996.

Tweed, Thomas A. *Our Lady of the Exile: Diasporic Religion at a Cuban Catholic Shrine in Miami.* New York: Oxford University Press, 1997.

Vizcaíno, Father Mario, Sch.P. *La Virgen de la Caridad: Patrona de Cuba.* Miami: Instituto Pastoral del Sureste, n.d.

Wakefield, Charito Calvachi. *Navidad Latinoamericana/Latin American Christmas.* Lancaster, Pennsylvania: Latin American Creations Publishing, 1997.

Directory of Latino Organizations in the United States

Latino cultural organizations could not be identified in some states, in which cases the next closest state is listed.

ALASKA
Latin Dance Social Club
4110 Northstar
Ancorage, AK 99503
(907) 563-6940

ALABAMA
see Tennessee

ARIZONA
Comité de Festividades Mexicanos de
    Tucson (Mexican Festival Committee
    of Tucson)
4652 North Camino Aire Fresco

Tucson, AZ 85705
(520) 292-9326

ARKANSAS
El Hispano
Rudy Lopez
514 Beaconsfield Road
Sherwood, AR 72120
(501) 945-7165

CALIFORNIA

Plaza de la Raza
3540 North Mission Rd.
Los Angeles, CA 90031
(323) 223-2475

Self-Help Graphics
3802 Cesar E. Chavez Avenue
Los Angeles, CA 90063
(323) 881-6444

Mission Cultural Center for Latino Arts
2868 Mission Street
San Francisco, CA 94110
(415) 821-1155

Galería de la Raza
2857 24th Street
San Francisco, CA 94110
(415) 826-8009

Mexican Heritage Plaza/Centro Cultural
de San Jose
1700 Alum Rock Avenue
San Jose, CA 95116
(408) 928-5500

COLORADO

Chicano Humanities and Arts Council
(CHAC)

772 Santa Fe Drive
Denver, CO 80204
(303) 571-0440

CONNECTICUT

Fernando Betancourt
State Commission on Latino and Puerto
Rican Affairs
18 Trinity St
Hartford, CT 06106
(860) 240-8330

Institute for the Hispanic Family
80 Jefferson St. # 1
Hartford, CT 06106
(860) 527-1124

DELAWARE

Dover District Hispanic Ministries
107 S. Front Street
Georgetown, DE 19947
(302) 855-9161

El Centro Cultural
P.O. Box 347
Georgetown, DE 19947
(302) 645-6575

FLORIDA

Manuel Toro (*La Prensa* Newspaper)
Fundacion Cultural Hispana/Hispanic
  Cultural Foundation
685 South C.R. 427
Longwood, FL 32750-6403
(407) 767-0070

Kiwanis Club of Little Havana
701 S.W. 27 Avenue, Ste. 900
Miami, Florida 33135
(305) 644-8888

GEORGIA

Latin American Association
2665 Buford Highway
Atlanta, GA 30324
(404) 638-1800

HAWAII

Centro Hispano/Hispanic Center of
  Hawaii
2044 S Beretania St. # 2
Honolulu, HI 96826
(808) 941-5216

Puerto Rican Association of Hawaii
1249 N. School St.
Honolulu, HI 96817
(808) 847-2751

IDAHO

Hispanic Affairs Commission
5460 West Franklin Rd Ste.B
Boise, ID 83705
(208) 334-3776

ILLINOIS

International Latino Cultural Center of
  Chicago
600 South Michigan Avenue
Chicago, IL 60605-1996
(312) 431-1330

Casa Aztlán
1831 South Racine
Chicago, IL 60608
(312) 666-5508

Mexican Fine Arts Center
1852 W 19th St
Chicago, IL 60608
(312) 738-1503

Humbolt Park Hispanic Church
1733 N Kedvale Ave
Chicago, IL 60639
(773) 235-0758

INDIANA

Fiesta Indianapolis
P.O. Box 40775
Indianapolis, IN 46240
(317) 767-5312

IOWA

Latino Affairs Division
Lucas State Office Building
Des Moines, IA 50319
(515) 281-4080

Los Amigos Club
P.O. Box 5674
Cedar Rapids, IA 52406-5674
(319) 362-7606

KANSAS

Committee on Hispanic Affairs
1430 S.W. Topeka Blvd.
Topeka, KS 66612
(785) 296-3465

KENTUCKY

see Indiana

LOUISIANA

Mensaje Festival
#4 Dauterive Court

Kenner, LA 70065
(504) 467-5245

MAINE

see Massachusetts

MASSACHUSETTS

Centro Latino de Chelsea, Inc.
267 Broadway
Chelsea, MA 02150
(617) 884-3238

MARYLAND

Federation of Hispanic Organizations of
    Maryland, Inc.
P.O. Box 25915
Baltimore, MD 21224
(410) 931-1640

MICHIGAN

Mexicantown Development Corp.
2630 Bagley St
Detroit, MI 48216
(313) 967-9898

Hispanic Center of Western Michigan
730 Grandville Ave., SW
Grand Rapids,
MI 49503
(616) 742-0200

MINNESOTA

Chicano/Latino Affairs Council
555 Park, Suite 210
St. Paul, MN 55103
(651) 296-9587

MISSISSIPPI

Trinity Mission Center
430 Hillsboro St
Forest, MS 39074
(601) 469-1346

MISSOURI

Greater Kansas City Hispanic Heritage
Committee, Inc.
10430 Askew Avenue
Kansas City, MO 64137-1517
(816) 765-1992

MONTANA

Las Flores Latinas
Arlene Zepeda de Walker
685 Sunset Blvd.
Calispell, MT 59901
(406) 752-6300

NEBRASKA

Hispanic Community Center/Centro de
la Comunidad Hispana
2300 'O' Street

Lincoln, NE 68510
(402) 474-3950

NEVADA

Rafael Rivera Community Center
2900 East Stuart
Las Vegas, NV 89101
(702) 229-4600

NEW JERSEY

Parada San Juan Baustista
P.O. Box 2908
Camden, NJ 08101
(856) 365-8888

NEW MEXICO

National Hispanic Cultural Center of
New Mexico
1701 4th Street, S.W.
Albuquerque, NM 87102
(505) 246-2261, fax (505) 246-2613

NEW YORK

Association of Hispanic Arts Inc.
250 W. 26th St, Fourth floor
New York, NY 10001
(212) 727-7227

El Museo del Barrio
1230 Fifth Avenue
New York, NY 10029-4496
(212) 831-7272

The Spanish Institute
684 Park Avenue
New York, NY 10021
(212) 628-0420

Westchester Hispanic Coalition, Inc.
46 Waller Ave.
White Plains, NY 10605
(914) 948-8466

NORTH CAROLINA
El Centro Hispano
1515 Mockingbird Lane # 540
Charlotte, NC 28209
(704) 529-1050

Latin American Coalition
322 Hawthorn Lane
Charlotte, NC 28204
(704) 333-5447

NORTH DAKOTA
see Minnesota

OHIO
Hispanic Community Center
4724 Byeszille Blvd.
Dayton, OH 45431
(937) 256-2233

OKLAHOMA
Hispanic Connection
1503 1/2 South Denver
Tulsa, OK 74119
(918) 835-6816

OREGON
Oregon Council for Hispanic
    Advancement
108 N.W 9th Ave Ste. 201
Portland, OR 97209
(503) 228-4131

PENNSYLVANIA
Mexican Cultural Center
111 South Independence Mall E
    Ste. 1010
Bourse Building
Philadelphia, PA 19106
(215) 592-0410

Council of Spanish Speaking
Organizations, Inc. (Concilio)
705-09 N. Franklin Street
Philadelphia, PA 19123
(215) 627-3100

RHODE ISLAND
Center for Hispanic Policy
421 Elmwood Ave
Providence, RI 02907
(401) 467-0111

SOUTH CAROLINA
see North Carolina

SOUTH DAKOTA
see Minnesota

TENNESSEE
Tennessee Latino
2608 Nolensville Rd. # C
Nashville, TN 37211
(615) 831-9030

TEXAS
Guadalupe Cultural Arts Center
1300 Guadalupe St.
San Antonio, TX 78207-5519
(210) 271-3151

National Association of Latino Arts and
Culture (NALAC)
3618 W. Commerce, Ste. 100
San Antonio, TX 78207
(210) 432-3982

Lubbock Centro Aztlan
1502 Ave. M
Lubbock, TX 79401
(806) 763-3841

Institute of Hispanic Culture
3315 Sul Ross
Houston, TX 77098
(713) 528-1492

Mexican Cultural Center
2917 Swiss Avenue
Dallas, TX 75204
(214) 824-9981

UTAH
State Office of Hispanic Affairs
324 S State St # 500
Salt Lake City, UT 84114
(801) 538-8634

VERMONT
see Massachusetts

VIRGINIA

Comité Hispano de Virginia/Hispanic
   Committee of Virginia
5827 Columbia Pike, Ste. 200
Falls Church, VA 22041
(703) 671-5666

WASHINGTON

El Centro De La Raza
2524 16th Ave S
Seattle, WA 98144
(206) 329-9442

WEST VIRGINIA

National Organization for the
   Advancement of Hispanics
2217 Princess Anne St
Fredericksburg, VA 22401
(540) 372-3437

WISCONSIN

Centro Guadalupe
1862 Beld St
Madison, WI 53713
(608) 255-8471

Centro de la Comunidad Unida-United
   Community Center
1028 S. 9th Street
Milwaukee, WI 53204
(414) 384-3100

WYOMING

see Colorado

WASHINGTON, DC

Centro de Arte
3047 15th St NW
Washington, DC 20009
(202) 588-5143

National Council of la Raza
1111 19th Street, N.W., Ste. 1000
Washington, DC 20036
(202) 785-1670